CONTENTS

J. M. Loughridge

May 20th, 1984.

FOREWORD

The papers published in this volume were given at the
conference 'Foreign influences on German: Past and Present' held
at the University of York from 28-30 March 1983.   The conference
was organised jointly by the Department of Language, University of
York, and the Goethe Institute in York.   I should like to thank
the past director of the Goethe Institute, Hanno Martin, for
arranging the conference and his successor Claudia Volkmar for
seeing it through and Catherine Arnott of the Goethe Institute for
invaluable organizational help.   Through funding by the Goethe
Institute we were able to invite Dr. Alan Kirkness and Dr. Gerhard
Stickel from Mannheim, Prof. Ekkehard König from Hanover and
Prof. John Hawkins fron Nijmegen.   All the papers given at the
conference have been reproduced here except for Prof. König's
'Concessive expressions in German: foreign influence or universal
affinity?' and Prof. Hawkins' 'English and German syntax in contact:
some general features of contrast and influence'.

I should like to thank all the participants who, by their
contributions in formal or informal discussion, helped to mould
the papers in their published form.

I should like to thank Mrs. Muriel Wood for her careful
typing of the manuscript.

Last, but not least, I should like to thank my wife Jenny
and my two sons for allowing me to dedicate my time to the
conference.

Department of Language,   Charles V.J. Russ
University of York

ISBN O 947584 O2 1

Printed by PDC Copyprint,
27 Woodside Place, Glasgow.

ALIENS, DENIZENS, HYBRIDS AND NATIVES: FOREIGN INFLUENCE ON THE
ETYMOLOGICAL STRUCTURE OF GERMAN VOCABULARY

Alan Kirkness
(Institut für deutsche Sprache, Mannheim)

My purpose in this paper[1] is to demonstrate that the traditional view of the etymological structure of German vocabulary is
untenable and to indicate briefly how this structure could perhaps
be described more adequately. To this end, I shall re-examine
the question of foreign lexical influence on German and then
draw some untraditional conclusions from this re-examination.
In particular, I hope to debunk the traditional concept of a
foreignism (*Fremdwort*).

Allow me to begin with a few preliminary remarks. Please
don't expect the presentation of a water-tight case with all
the loose ends neatly tied. Expect rather a provisional report
on work in progress or thoughts in gestation that is designed to
elicit your comments and criticism. My examination of various
individual points will not necessarily always be novel but I hope
that the conclusions drawn might provoke a lively discussion. I
shall be looking at where German words come from, especially those
allegedly, supposedly, or in fact, from abroad. The use of the
phrase 'etymological structure' above suggests that there is a
pattern over- or underlying random individual etymologies, and
that it is my concern to proceed from the trees to the wood. Put
very briefly, the task of etymology is to describe the origin (and
history) of both form and content of a lexical item with regard
to related items (i.e. word families and semantic fields) and to
equivalents in related languages. 'German' refers to present-
day standard German, especially in its written form, in other
words: to the supraregional standardised usage of the German
language community in general as used, for example, in the mass
media and as learned by foreign students abroad. Thus problems
peculiar to the dialects, for example, to spoken usage or to
the historical stages of German as such will not be treated here.
This is a lexicological study, and phonological or syntactic
features, for instance, will not be considered *per se*, but only

- 1 -

in relation to lexical ones. I shan't attempt to give even a
working definition of 'word', but content myself with two statements that should hardly raise any linguist's eyebrows:

1. As linguistic entities, words are two-faced, a symbiosis
    of form and content, of *signifiant* and *signifié*. Put
    differently: the linguistic sign is bilateral.

2. Words are used in a wide variety of co- and contexts, in
    varying relations to other words and in different communi-
    cative situations. Chomsky's ideal speaker/hearer in a
    homogenous language community is, I believe, a convenient
    fiction of the past. Lasswell's formula

        Who
        Says What
        In Which Channel
        To Whom
        With What Effect?

could be, I believe, the inconvenient truth of the future.[2]

Present-day lexicology sits, in my view, uneasily between
the two. In other words: to be the very model of a modern lexi-
cologist, one has at least to consider matters formal, semantic,
syntagmatic, paradigmatic and pragmatic. The implications of
such a tall order for lexicology will become only partly clear
here, as this is an etymological study. But they cannot be
ignored, as they are in the traditional view of foreign influence
on German vocabulary. Which brings me back to my subject. Let
me end these preliminaries on a terminological note by introducing first the German counterparts of the aliens, denizens,
hybrids and natives in the title.[3] In academic circles they go
by the name of *Fremdwörter, Lehnwörter, hybride* or *Mischbildungen*
or *Teillehnwörter* and *Erbwörter*. The community at large distinguishes merely between foreignisms (*Fremdwörter*) and German
words (*deutsche Wörter*). 'Foreignism' will be used here as a
generic term covering roughly aliens, denizens (and hybrids).
A critique of this concept is my main concern in this paper.
'Foreign word' I regard as a translation of *fremdes Wort* for a
word used in German rather as a quotation to refer to some
foreign object, institution, concept etc. properly restricted
to a non-German context in the widest sense. A similar term is

exoticism (*Exotismus*).   'Foreign word' will not be used here as
its referent does not belong to the German lexical system and
can thus fairly be disregarded in any consideration of etymological
structure.   It is truly an alien, as opposed to the foreignisms,
which are not.   I may emphasize here that I am interested primarily in the categories of foreign lexical influence on German and
less concerned with the terms used as labels for those categories.

I shall proceed in the following steps:

1. A survey of the source material available on foreign
influence on German - past and present.
2. An exposition of the traditional view of the etymological structure of German vocabulary in the light of
foreign influence.
3. A detailed critical examination of this view.
4. An outline of a different view that takes both word form
and word content into account.
5. Some concluding remarks on the academic and non-academic
point of a new look at the etymological structure of German
vocabulary in the light of foreign influence.

It is a truism that the history of German vocabulary is *inter
alia* a history of foreign influence, as even the most cursory
glance at any history of the language will confirm.   So it is
hardly surprising that this influence should have attracted a
lot of attention.   Quantitatively at least, we cannot complain
about lack of source material.   To start with there is the centuries old puristic literature.   A dead letter academically,
purism still has its supporters in the community at large.
Certainly the foreignism has its detractors, as the endless discussion on, i.e. against, foreignisms in the press indicates.
Such literature is important as a reflection of the popular
attitudes to foreign lexical influence nurtured mainly in the
schools.   I shall return to this topic at the end.   Closely
related, indeed often a concomitant, is the equally old, if not
older tradition of the dictionary of foreignisms, which dates
from 1571.   Surely no country can have anywhere near as many such
dictionaries as Germany: between 1800 and 1945, for example,
after a gradual build up in the 17th and 18th centuries, some 300
different dictionaries appeared and many saw numerous editions.

Even today they come in a bewildering array of shapes and sizes, prices and content. The answer to the question, why this is so and why until very recently foreignisms were generally banned on principle from German dictionaries, would be most revealing. The causes of this separate tradition are not fully researched. Purism is certainly a major factor. One consequence seems to me to be clear: by banning foreignisms to the ghetto of a separate dictionary, by keeping them apart from the linguistic mainstream, i.e. by treating them as aliens, as non-German, one has helped ensure that they remain - seemingly - just that, namely non-German aliens, and obstruct any process of assimilation and acceptance. This in turn becomes a reason, or rather a pretext, for treating them separately, and a vicious circle is complete. To overstate somewhat, I would suggest that indirectly in the long term dictionaries of foreignisms cause as many problems of understanding as they may solve directly in the short term. Be that as it may, as source material for our subject they must be treated with reserved caution. Of value are Sanders (1871) and Kehrein (1876) because of their textual examples, and particularly the historical Deutsches Fremdwörterbuch begun by Hans Schulz, continued by Otto Basler, and recently completed in the Institut für deutsche Sprache in Mannheim. Occasionally, however, they shed unexpected - and unwitting? - light on German word formation on a foreign basis, especially on derivatives and neo-Latin combinations. Judging from our work on Schulz/Basler, I strongly suspect that lexicographers such as Karl Heyse have systematically 'completed' word families by coining 'missing' members, 'missing' in the sense that we had no contemporary textual examples for them in our material and/or that there was no traceable term in a foreign language that could have been the source of a borrowing. This suspicion applies above all to Latinisms, for patterns of word formation on a Latin basis were well established in German by the early 19th century, as Heyse's coining and coinages testify. But more of this later. The general historical and etymological dictionaries of German leave a tremendous amount to be desired in their treatment of foreignisms - any improvement is recent and partial. The lexicographical treatment of loan substitutions (*inneres Lehngut* or *Lehnprägungen*) is even more

piecemeal and unsatisfactory.   Indeed, the general and technical
German encyclopaedias are much more fruitful and reliable source
material on foreignisms than language dictionaries in the narrow
sense, especially as regards the history of meaning.   But the
lexicographical treatment of foreign influences on German is a
separate study and I have become sidetracked.

Invaluable as source material is a series of monographs de-
voted to individual key concepts or words or word families, e.g.
Evolution, Kultur, Revolution, Sozialismus, Technik or *Zivili-
sation*.   Regrettably, the list of such key words is many times
bigger than the number of available studies.   The same applies
generally to monographs on the use of foreignisms in individual
authors, such as Wolfram, Murner, Fischart, Schiller, Goethe,
Fontane and others, and to historical studies on foreign influence
on languages for special purposes (at a particular time), such as
school terminology, commerce and mathematics.   Better known are
studies on the influence of individual donor languages (at a given
epoch), viz. Spanish, Italian, Russian and other Slavonic languages,
the languages of the New World, and in particular Latin and Greek,
French and English.   The influence of English - including American
and what we might call International English - since 1945 is an
evergrowing research industry in itself, and the years from 1640
to 1815 have been well covered.   However, to my knowledge, reliable in-depth studies of the period 1815 to 1945 have yet to
appear.   Interestingly, the question of English loan substitutions
has received a deal of attention.   As regards French influence
on Middle and New High German, we are well served for the period
up to 1735 (and on to 1748), but the latter part of the 18th and
the whole of the 19th century have yet to be treated in depth.
These are important gaps, but much more serious are the gaps in
the research literature on the classical languages, less so on
the direct influence of Greek than on the constant and all-per-
vasive influence of Latin and Neo-Latin (including Greek).   For
me, modern standard German in its written form, subject as it is
particularly and increasingly to lexical influences resulting
from the explosion of knowledge, especially in science and technology, and from international news coverage in all fields, can
be fairly, if oversimply, described as latinised Germanic.   More

particularly, academic German, which I take to be a form of written standard German, has a full share in the common European Latin and Neo-Latin patrimony. But the traditional view of the etymological structure of German vocabulary has not taken this nearly far enough into account. Partly because the source material is so uneven in both quantity and quality. We are relatively well informed on Latin loan substitutions in the Old High German period, but only the tip of the Middle High German iceberg has been revealed: The language of administration in the widest sense and the idioms of scholasticism and mysticism still have secrets to yield. As regards the New High German period, we have, to give but four examples, no systematic study of how German took over from (Neo-)Latin as an academic language or of the contribution of academic German, as opposed to literary German in a more restricted sense, to the genesis of modern Standard German; we have no modern systematic studies on (Neo-)Latin, i.e. European, influence on the semantic structure of German; we have no systematic treatment of the (Neo-)Latin, i.e. European, word formation patterns and elements so characteristic of German academic usage; and we have no systematic diachronic studies on the phonological or morphological subsystems constituted by German Latinisms - whether borrowed into or coined in German - or on their role in shaping German phonological and morphological structure in such a way that it has become receptive to Gallicisms and Anglicisms, especially those of Latin origin. These four fields are all, I maintain, directly relevant to our subject. But until we have more than just a few isolated studies on specific and restricted topics this must remain an assertion based on piecemeal evidence, rather than a statement of demonstrable fact.

To sum up: For all the wealth of source material available, our view of the etymological structure of German vocabulary in the light of foreign influence is necessarily incomplete. The most pressing need is for further studies on French and English, and above all for further research into the influence of (Neo-)Latin since the age of Humanism and the Renaissance. Such research would, I am convinced, provide a corrective to the traditional view of the structure under discussion, to which I now turn. Needless to say, the material reviewed above has served as a basis for innumerable discussions on foreign lexical influence, including typologies of loan substitutions and importations (*inneres und äußeres Lehngut*). The traditional view of the latter concerns us here. In presenting this view, I shall translate as literally as possible what might be considered an enlightened statement of it designed specifically for use in schools. I have chosen to fly under borrowed colours, as it were, in an attempt to prevent my personal bias obtruding at this stage. The version is by Gerhard Augst (translation AK):

> Linguists distinguish etymologically between
>
> natives (*Erbwörter*): *Haus, Mann, Fisch, Wand, Herzog*
> aliens (*Fremdwörter*): *Idee, interessant, Chirurg, Fight*
> denizens (*Lehnwörter*): *Fenster, Nase, Opfer, Streik, preisen*
>
> Natives are words that have been handed down to us from Indogermanic and later through Germanic, Old, Middle and New High German up to the present day. Also included here are neologisms (*Wortneuschöpfungen*). Aliens and denizens stem from foreign languages; some time between Indogermanic and today they have penetrated into the Germanic or German language. While the aliens have largely preserved their foreign form as regards spelling, pronunciation and morphology, the denizens have largely adapted to the external form (*signifiant*) of the natives, with the result that the layman is unable to distinguish them from German words.

Augst continues with the following commentary:

> Two conclusions may be drawn from these definitions:
>
> 1. The boundaries between alien and denizen are fluid. They depend on how clearly the speaker is conscious of the *signifiant* structure (the external form) of natives and on what context the words are used in. Clearly there is differing importance attached to the various possibilities for deviation (spelling, pronunciation, morphology).
>
> 2. The historically schooled linguist and the layman with little knowledge of the etymology of words arrive at different classifications of the vocabulary:
>
>   Linguist: natives // denizens / aliens
>   Layman: German words // foreignisms
>
> It may be said that in general the layman takes natives and denizens together as German words. However, deviations are possible in two respects:
>
> 1. There are some words which as regards external form do not differ at all from German words, but which

the speaker takes to be aliens nonetheless because
he knows that they stem from a foreign language
(e.g. *killen, Nigger, konisch*). Generalising
somewhat: almost every speaker knows that apart
from his (native) language there are other languages
and that - in some cases more than others - words
from these languages penetrate into his own.
Almost every German knows 'a few snatches' of
English.

2. On the other hand, there are words which are natives
as regards etymology, but which many speakers
classify as aliens because of their external form
(e.g. *Bovist, Pirol, Balsam, Efeu*). Synchronically,
the speaker apparently acts on the assumption that
the words of his mother tongue are constructed
according to certain structural laws.

In view of the fact that the speaker does not pick out all
those natives which contradict the synchronic structural
laws in one or more respects (e.g. *Forelle, Kobold, Hornisse*),
we can conclude that both approaches are complementary.
Many foreignisms, in contrast to German words, can lead to
secondary 'foreign' formation principles according to which
the speaker can classify other words which he had not heard
before or which make him unsure as aliens, as in the case
of *Bovist* with the typically French stress on the last
syllable and the French ending *-ist*.

Thus the most important finding of this section is that a
strict distinction must be made between a historical-genetic
[or diachronic] description and an understanding at a given
stage of a language. In addition, the knowledge a normal
speaker has of his (native) language must be clearly
separated from what the linguist knows about a language.
As regards foreignisms, this leads to different classifications.[4]

Thus far Gerhard Augst and the traditional view. I have
called his exposition enlightened *inter alia* because it recog-
nises the fact that the linguist's and the layman's approaches
are different - albeit much too little so - and the need to avoid
confusing diachrony and synchrony, etymology and word form; and
because it points to the all too obvious fact that the layman's
approach is inconsistent and contradictory. The linguist's
traditional approach is, I maintain, equally untenable. To sub-
stantiate this claim, I want first to look in turn at the two
main features of the traditional view of foreignisms, i.e. of
aliens and denizens (and hybrids):

1. That they have been taken over from foreign languages.

2. That the aliens as opposed to the denizens have not (yet) been formally assimilated or, in other words, that the distinction made between aliens and denizens rests on formal assimilation (or lack of it).

The first claim is demonstrably false. There is no question that German has at all stages of its development borrowed words from abroad, or more accurately: that German native speakers have at all stages in the history of German used words taken over from foreign languages in their texts. There is equally no question that many of the words considered to be foreignisms have not been borrowed from any other language. What was the donor language, for instance, in the case of *Blamage, Dressman, Raffinesse, Renommage, Showmaster* or *Twen*? Neither French nor English for sure. And yet all these words are considered to be foreignisms, if we may take the dictionaries of foreignisms as a guide to what foreignisms are. And for lack of empirical field work based on sound methodological principles we must accept such dictionaries as the best guide we have. In the historical Deutsches Fremdwörterbuch known as Schulz/Basler, the letter *S* has some 1267 headwords either as main- or sub-entries. Of these approximately 750 have no direct model, and often not even an equivalent, in any foreign language that might have been a possible donor. The letter *T* has some 850 entries, of which 550 are not demonstrably borrowings (*Wortentlehnungen*). In other words, some 65% of the foreignisms registered here have not been taken over from other languages. And this is the only dictionary of foreignisms that is primarily diachronic and etymological in approach and that is based on a large number of historical textual examples. The same non-borrowed foreignisms can also be found, allowing for a natural variation according to the aims and principles of the various works, in other contemporary dictionaries of foreignisms. Either the dictionaries are sadly astray, and even the most perfunctory of polls or questionnaires on what a foreignism is would confirm that this is not the case. Or the traditional definition of a foreignism, that it has been taken over from a foreign language, is false. This is the only conclusion we can reasonably come to.

If many, perhaps even the majority of, foreignisms are demonstrably or not demonstrably borrowings from other languages,
what are they? Let us consider the following classes of words that
can be found in German dictionaries of foreignisms.   The classification stems from Elisabeth Link[5]:

- derivatives with the name of a non-German as one component and
  and either a borrowed or indigenous affix as another:
  platonisch, salomonisch, Platonismus;

- derivatives with the name of a German as one component and a
  borrowed affix as another: *Marxismus, Draisine, kafkaesk;*

- derivatives with a borrowed component as base and an indigenous
  component as affix: *Raffiniertheit, Borniertheit, Regulierung;*

- derivatives with an indigenous component as base and a borrowed
  component as affix: *Bummelant, Schwulität, halbieren, Exkönig,
  nachspionieron;*

- derivatives with borrowed components as base and as affix but
  without a demonstrable model in a foreign language: *Blamage,
  rentabel, Rentabilität, Rasanz;*

- clippings based on foreignisms: *Pulli, Profi, Sozi* (or even on
  foreign words: *Twen,* cf. Engl. *twenty*);

- compounds with a borrowed component as determinant and an indigenous component as determinatum: *Reaktionszeit, Radikalenerlaß,
  Veloursleder, Kontaktmann;*

- compounds with a borrowed component as determinatum and an indigenous component as determinant: *Volksrepublik, Jugendkrimina-
  lität, Dirndllook;*

- compounds with borrowed components as determinant and determinatum but without a demonstrable model in a foreign language,
  whereby the components may both/all occur on their own as morphological items in German: *Parteiprogramm, Reaktionsmechanismus,*
  or whereby not all the components occur on their own: *Showmaster,
  Dressman;*

- combinations resembling derivatives and/or compounds with partly
  or, for the most part, wholly borrowed components (especially
  from (Neo-)Latin) but without a demonstrable model in a foreign

language: *Schizophrenie, Technolekt, Politologie, Politrocker, Politökonom, Ökotopia, Europtreff, Euroscheck, Roseomanie, Tretomanie, Spielothek, Grusical, Startomatic, Telefonmobil, Wohnmobil;*

- syntagmas with borrowed components but without a demonstrable model in a foreign language: *va banque.*

The items in these classes have not been (demonstrably) borrowed from abroad, but coined in German, mainly on a foreign/borrowed basis. They may be designated as loan coinages (*Lehnwortbildungen*), a term that is more apposite and less suggestive than the one often used for words like *Blamage, Twen* etc., namely pseudo-borrowing (*Schein-, Pseudoentlehnung*). In many cases, especially as regards derivatives with Latin components and the combinations on a (Neo-)Latin basis, the possibility of borrowing cannot be excluded, for most of the relevant word formation elements and patterns are common to all the main West European languages and in many cases the coinages are too. On occasion, the possibility of polygenesis must also be taken into account. Difficulties in deciding on borrowing, coinage in the domestic German tradition, or polygenesis, are caused partly by the fact that such coining on a foreign basis has until very recently been very largely ignored by German linguists. Most available studies are piecemeal and based on insufficient textual evidence. We have little reliable information on when such elements and patterns have become productive in German. Judging again from our work on Schulz/Basler, I should say that most of the patterns and many of the elements had become productive before the end of the 18th century. But for the time being this is little more than an informed guess. To my knowledge, foreignisms are subject to no particular distribution restrictions but 'behave' just like natives when it comes to compounds of the determinant - determinatum type. These are the subject of a detailed study at present being made in Innsbruck. The dictionaries of foreignisms register only a fraction of even the fully lexicalised compounds of the three types listed above. Not surprisingly, those compounded from borrowed components alone are most frequently found. The other two classes are known generally, and pejoratively, as hybrids. Their treatment in the dictionaries of foreignisms varies widely and we have no other material on whether they are generally regarded as foreign or not. I shall return to the hybrids later. 'The foreign element in German derivational morphology', to quote a title[6], has recently been studied in depth in Innsbruck, at least as far as present-day Standard German is concerned[7]. The Innsbruck study also breaks with the practice in traditional manuals on word formation of treating the foreign element, if it is treated at all, separately from German derivational morphemes. We may note in passing that this is also the rule in other areas of linguistic description such as phonology and, as we have seen, lexicography. The suggestion is, of course, that elements of foreign origin are non-German in spite of their everyday use by Germans alone solely to and for Germans, i.e. in a monolingual situation. The layman's polarisation (of vocabulary) into foreign and German as noted earlier pervades all levels of linguistic description. Changes for the better are few and recent. But back to derivational morphology: On occasion the terminology changes to foreign and native (*heimisch*), but the treatment remains separate. Diachronic aspects have yet to be studied extensively or intensively, as has the dominant role of the foreign basis of coining in general educated and in academic usage and in many languages for special purposes - at present we have only a few courses on scientific, especially medical terminology to rely on. The neglect of what I have called combinations on a (Neo-) Latin basis is virtually total, even though they have been a major constitutive feature of academic German since at least the 18th century. The standard division of word combinations into compounds and derivatives break down here, but no theory of the linguistic sign in German has yet, to my knowledge, taken account of the fact.

A Mannheim project with the title 'Synchronic and Diachronic Studies on Word Formation on a Foreign Basis in German (Loan Coining)' is designed to meet this deficit. Its findings will, I am convinced, necessitate a reassessment of German derivational and combinational morphology and demonstrate conclusively that

the traditional view, a foreignism is a borrowing, is untenable.
Too many so-called foreignisms are coined in German, and often
in German alone. They receive full coverage in practically all
dictionaries of foreignisms, regardless of whether they're labelled aliens or, less frequently, hybrids. But that such coinages
should be labelled foreignisms in linguistic usage seems to me
at best unfounded, at worst absurd. They may belong to some
degree to the periphery of the standard language system and they
do form a subsystem of their own beside the native central system
of Germanic origin, but they are undoubtedly German and there is,
I believe, evidence to suggest that they have become at least as
productive as, if not more productive than, the native system in
present-day Standard German. The continuing Europeanisation of
latinised Germanic alias German is perhaps nowhere more apparent
than in the area of word formation.

        I turn now to the second aspect of the traditional view of
foreignisms, the distinction between aliens and denizens on the
basis of the formal assimilation of the latter. One cannot say
that this distinction is false, in the sense that the equation
foreignisms = borrowing clearly is. But it is, I submit, generally unhelpful and, in the light of my opening remarks on modern
lexicology, linguistically inadequate and antiquated. As you
know, the distinction between alien and denizen has been the subject of much discussion in the literature. There seems to be
consensus that the boundaries are fluid, but the consequences
drawn therefrom are very different - some retain the distinction,
others give it up. The resulting terminological confusion is at
times considerable. In giving my own view, I shall attempt not
merely to rehash the old arguments. They provide, however, a
useful starting point, for they indicate that denizens fall into
two groups. Only the second group is controversial. This indicates that there are denizens and denizens and that it might be
interesting to see what distinguishes denizen from denizen, let
alone from alien. Or, indeed, from native, as we have already
seen from Augst's commentary! But I shall not pursue that here,
except to say that it does throw into question the importance to

to be attached to isolated word forms. The first group consists
of words such as *Wein, Tisch, Mauer* and *Ziegel* or *Kirche, Priester*
opfern and *Bischof*, which, incidentally, are not to be found in
any dictionary of foreignisms, even though they are borrowed.
The second group includes words like *Rang, Raster, Rate, Rose,*
Sport, Streik and *Titel*, which may or may not be found in dictionaries of foreignisms as the case may be. The salient difference
between the two, as I see it, is the time of borrowing. The
former either pre-date or accompany the development from Germanic
to (Old High) German that took place in the period from the 5th
to the late 8th and 9th centuries. The latter were borrowed
later, and practically all of them were borrowed much later, most
in the New High German period. We may note further that the
former date from a period from which very few aliens have been
handed down, and most of them seem to have been borrowed very late
in the period, at least as far as I can see at the moment. With
the latter this is not the case. Indeed, quite the reverse.
And this difference seems to me to be important. It can be interpreted as a statement on the structure of the recipient language
and on the attitudes of native speakers of that language to
borrowings. A transition occurs, and I must emphasise the element of speculation here, in the latter part of the 12th century
and is marked linguistically by the appearance of verbs ending in
-ier-en. The verbal suffix *-ier(-en)* borrowed from the French
is still extremely productive today in its original form. From
the Middle High German period on, both aliens and denizens in the
traditional sense still survive, and it would be interesting to
investigate by means of a questionnaire which of the surviving
words from *Abenteuer* to *Reliquie* the language community considers
aliens and which denizens. The general consensus seems to be
that the denizens predominate. In the New High German period,
especially with the onset of printing and the new importance of
the written and printed word, the situation is radically different
with the aliens clearly predominant. Perhaps the transition I
have spoken of is better located here? In other words, to state
the obvious, there is a world of difference between Old High

German and New High German in the treatment of borrowings. For
this reason, it is surely unconvincing to see in the denizens of
the first group the model for a development from alien to denizen
by means of formal assimilation (to the native structure) that
applies to those in the second group, or to see in denizens former
aliens. Language development in New High German times follows
different laws, for not only is the language community a totally
different, ever changing one, but the structure of the recipient
language is also very different and ever changing. And one of
the major factors determining this change is, to state the obvious
again, foreign influence. Mention of the innumerable loan coinages of the New High German period discussed earlier should suffice here to underline the point. Such loan coinages, for example
and in particular the derivatives and combinations coined on a
Latin basis, now come 'ready made', as it were, in their final
German form and do not undergo further formal assimilation. Indeed,
I think it fair to say that this is now true of all Latinisms in
the widest sense, whether borrowed from (Neo-)Latin, French or
English, or coined in German. This was not always the case, hence
my use of 'now'. In the 15th and 16th centuries and on into the
17th, there was a deal of fluctuation and interchange between the
set of native elements ultimately of Germanic origin and the set
of foreign elements mainly of Latin or Romance origin, enough at
any rate to make an integrated system seem a possibility. However,
in the 17th and 18th centuries, with the development of the notion,
if not the name of a foreignism - the term *Fremdwort* dates from
the beginning of the 19th century - and with the onset of organised
purism in the sense of an anti-foreignism campaign, the two sets
largely parted company. Crossfertilisation decreased, the sta-
bility of the independent sets increased. Here again, we can see
evidence of a transition in speakers' attitudes and of changes in
language structure. The Latin set can now be regarded as a fully
integrated subsystem in German with a stable phonological, orthographical and morphological structure, so that Latinisms now pose
few problems of gender, inflection or accent etc. to those German
speakers familiar with this subsystem. That they form a small

minority is another question. This latinised subsystem constitutes for me one of the vital differences between Germanic and
German, but it is one that the language community at large is
hardly conscious of and one whose importance linguists have, in
my view, underestimated. The consequences are clear: for the
majority of Germans, Latinisms are hard words, and one of the
reasons for this is that the Latinisms are for the majority of
Germans not morphologically motivated or transparent. But I'll
come back to this at the end. To return to aliens and denizens:
I suspect that borrowings from other languages, notably French,
may now be adapted to this foreign subsystem rather than to the
native one. I suspect further that this is perhaps less true
of the anglicisms, except of course those of Latin origin, but
that these are establishing formal patterns and structures of
their own. Be that as it may, complete formal assimilation to
native structure is no longer the natural 'fate' of foreignisms,
as it was of the borrowings in the pre-German and Old High German
periods. For this reason, I regard the denizens of our first
group as a class of their own. As far as the etymological structure of modern German is concerned, I personally am rather inclined
to consider them, in accordance with the layman's approach as
described by Augst, as natives and to extend the traditional view
of natives (*Erbwörter*) to include them alongside indigenous
Germanic words. But perhaps this underestimates too much the
constants in the development from Germanic to German that Stefan
Sonderegger has recently emphasised so strongly.[8]

As regards the denizens of our second group, on the other
hand, I can see no practical point in distinguishing between them
and aliens, quite apart from the fact that no one scholar has yet
succeeded, nor in my view will ever succeed, in convincing others
as to where the line is to be drawn or even what the formal
criteria are for drawing such a line. I can see no linguistic
justification for it either. The distinction as made tradition-
ally is based on a monolateral concept of the linguistic sign I
consider to be antiquated. An atomistic approach to isolated
word forms alone, or even to individual features of word form,

such as spelling or pronunciation as opposed to inflection for instance, such an approach can surely no longer be considered acceptable in modern lexicology? The main criticism to be levelled at the traditional division of foreignisms into aliens and denizens is that it considers only word forms, and leaves out of account word meanings, let alone the co- and contexts that words are used in.

Important consequences must be drawn for both the synchronic and the diachronic description of German vocabulary. In respect of synchrony, this point has been made very cogently by Peter von Polenz, so that I can rest content here by referring to him.[9] In respect of diachrony, the assimilation of word forms must be seen as but one aspect of a process involving word forms, word meanings and word use by which foreignisms, more particularly borrowed ones, are integrated into German vocabulary. Research on integration (*Integrationsforschung*) is in its infancy, but Horst Munske is pointing the way to an enlightened and enlightening future.[10] Integration may be interpreted for the moment as the movement of a foreignism or borrowing from the periphery towards the centre of the lexical system of German, whereby I am well aware of the difficulties in defining centre and periphery, system and subsystem etc. This movement can be traced in a number of variable features on different levels of linguistic description including phonology, morphology, syntax, semantics and pragmatics. A description of integration should consider questions such as what the word looks and sounds like at various stages of its development and, more importantly, given the fact that many foreignisms come formally 'ready made', who uses it to whom in what sense(s) and in what context(s). Among the features that should be examined in detail are orthography, pronunciation, gender, inflection, word formation (derivation, composition, and combination in the sense discussed earlier), set phrases and idioms, semantic change and development (borrowed as opposed to non-borrowed meanings, transferred and figurative usage, semantic fields, synonyms and antonyms, denotation and connotations), stylistics, frequency and distribution (spoken or written usage, colloquial - formal - technical usage, text-types,

social range etc.). Taken together the variable features make
up a scale which can be used to determine the degree of integration.
As it is a sliding scale, any findings must be regarded as relative,
liable to further change and differing interpretations. A word
that might be familiar to and actively used by one speaker may be
known to but not used by another and unknown even in the passive
competence of a third. Such variation will depend on age, social,
educational and professional background and on geographical and
political situation. Similarly, a word may have reached different
points along the scale according to the particular feature examined
in isolation, and the relative importance attached to structural,
semantic and distributional factors may well vary from one linguist
to another. The possible combinations and permutations are therefore legion. Differences in the degree of integration will be
just that, differences in degree, not in kind. For this reason,
a bipartite division such as that into aliens and denizens will be
impossible. It remains to be seen whether such an approach will
prove practicable, whether it is feasible, for instance, to distinguish between central and peripheral meanings; and it is not
surprising that integration studies have started with word forms.
The important thing is, however, to go beyond them.

Equally as important as the changes undergone by individual
foreignisms as they become more and more integrated into the system
of German are the changes in that system brought about by the
integration of foreignisms or by foreign influence in general,
e.g. additions to the phoneme and morpheme inventory, new plural
and derivational paradigms, the shifting relationship between
motivation and dissociation and alterations to and in semantic
fields. That new patterns and analogies have developed, and that
these alter the system into which new foreignisms are integrated
and that this in turn leads to changes in the process of integration,
has, I hope, become clear from the preceding discussion.

To sum up briefly: I do not accept the traditional distinction between aliens and denizens any more than I accept the
traditional concept of a foreignism. As regards our subject, the

traditional view gives an inadequate, one-sided view of the etymological structure of German vocabulary. Both the traditional
alien: denizen distinction and the traditional concept of a
foreignism are based, as I have indicated, solely on word forms.
This criticism must be regarded as a *sine qua non* of any academic
discussion on the question of foreignisms (*Fremdwortfrage*).

But what about the other side of the coin, word content or
word meaning, given that word form and word meaning are like the
two sides of a Möbius strip and must be considered together in
modern lexicology? I should like to turn now briefly to word
content, and begin with the bald statement that consideration of
matters semantic will act as a radical corrective to the traditional view of the etymological structure of German vocabulary.

Consideration of word content brings us first to the question
of loan substitution (*Lehnprägung*, or preferably *inneres Lehngut*),
research into which is well established as a branch of lexicology.
However, its findings have yet to influence traditional etymology
to any extent. Our knowledge of loan substitution in German is
uneven. In this respect, as in others, well researched Old High
German differs markedly from less well known Middle High German,
let alone from New High German, where we have only general studies
based on insufficient textual evidence; comments on specific
entries in historical German dictionaries, notably Grimm, which
reveal even words like *Geist, Gnade, Gott, gut, Sünde* and *Welt*,
which have never aroused puristic ire, in a new, 'foreign' light;
and more detailed and conclusive studies on individual words,
especially anglicisms. In addition, the puristic tradition of
substitute words (*Ersatzwörter* or *Verdeutschungen*) offers a rich
source of revealing material which must, however, be treated with
caution. The importance of loan substitution for German as a
European language has been eloquently argued and demonstrated by
Fritz Mauthner, but his Wörterbuch der Philosophie (1910/11) is
little known, and underlined by Werner Betz and his school in a
series of works on the impact of Latin on German, or rather
Germanic?, in the Old High German period. On the basis of this

work Betz evolved a typology and terminology of loan substitutions
that have become the basis for subsequent discussion on the subject.[11]
Betz defines his types with examples as follows - I quote from his
6th edition of Hermann Paul's Deutsches Wörterbuch and offer an
English term each time:

> *Lehnbedeutung* (loan meaning): 'von einem laut- oder
> bedeutungsähnlichen fremden Wort entliehene Bedeutung',
> cf. *realisieren* 'sich bewußt machen' - Engl. *realize,*
> *Geist - Fr. esprit;*
>
> *Lehnbildung* (loan shift): 'Neubildung in einer Sprache
> nach fremdem (inhaltlichem, formalem) Vorbild';
>
> *Lehnformung* (loan formation): 'Neubildung in einer Sprache
> nach fremdem formalem (und inhaltlichem) Vorbild';
>
> *Lehnprägung* (loan substitution): 'Neubildung oder
> Neubedeutung nach fremdem Vorbild';
>
> *Lehnschöpfung* (loan creation): 'Neubildung nach fremdem
> inhaltlichem Vorbild ohne formale Anlehnung'. cf.
> *Mundart - Dialekt;*
>
> *Lehnübersetzung* (loan translation): 'Glied-für-Glied-
> Nachbildung eines fremden Vorbilds', cf. *teilnehmen -*
> *participare;*
>
> *Lehnübertragung* (loan rendition): 'Teil-Nachbildung eines
> fremden Vorbildes', cf. *Vaterlang - patria.*

He groups loan translation and loan rendition together as loan
formation, loan formation and loan creation together as loan shift,
and uses loan substitution as a generic term to cover loan shift
and loan meaning. The following diagram makes the relationships
clear:

I shall not review the subsequent discussion here, as this
has been done at length in a recent (1975) work on the theory and
practice of loan substitution by Notburga Bäcker.[12] Bäcker evolves
her own typology on the basis of Betz, Einar Haugen, Manfred
Höfler and others and on the basis of an empirical study of English

loan substitutions in French sporting terminology.   She also goes
into the very considerable practical problems of how to recognise
and to classify loan substitutions.   Here I can but summarise the
main points I consider relevant to the question of lexical borrowing
as part of a new look at the etymological structure of German
vocabulary in the light of foreign influence.   In the preceding
discussion you will have noted, I trust, an increasing irritation
with the notion of a foreignism, deliberately reflected *inter alia*
in the use of the terms borrowing (*Wortentlehnung*) and loan coinage
(*Lehnwortbildung*).   While looking at types of lexical borrowing
more closely, I propose to discard the term foreignism as it ob-
scures important issues.   The term borrowing will also have to be
used more precisely.

According to whether word forms are taken over or replaced in
the process of borrowing, we can distinguish three main categories
of borrowings:

1. The donor language form is taken over or imported into
    the recipient language: loan word (*Lehnwort*).   That
    loan words, which I have been calling loosely borrowings
    up to now, undergo varying degrees of integration into
    German has already been discussed above.

2. The donor language form is taken over in part, in part
    replaced in the recipient language: loan blend (*Teil-
    lehnwort*).   Loan blends must by definition be complex
    morphological items, the component replaced may be a
    word or an affix.   The imported component is taken
    over at the time the loan blend is coined, i.e. it is
    an item new to the inventory of the recipient language.
    From this we must distinguish cases where an already
    borrowed word, a loan word, is used within the recipient
    language together with a native element to form a new
    complex morphological item.   Such cases are not
    borrowings.   The traditional term hybrid glosses over
    this important distinction.

3. The donor language form is replaced in the recipient
   language: loan substitution (*inneres Lehngut*). The
   term *Lehnprägung* is less suitable here as it suggests
   that a new word is coined. This is not always the
   case. Thus we can differentiate between those cases
   where a new word is coined in the recipient language:
   loan shift, and those where an already extant word of
   the recipient language is used and acquires a new
   meaning: loan meaning. Subtypes of loan meaning
   may be distinguished, but need not detain us here.
   Examples are *feuern* 'entlassen' after Engl. *fire*, *Ente*
   'Zeitungslüge' after Fr. *canard* or *realisieren* 'sich
   bewußt machen, kapieren' after Engl. *realise*. With
   realisieren in this sense it is a moot point whether
   it is better classified as a loan meaning, so that
   realisieren is regarded as being polysemous (cf. 'ver-
   wirklichen'), or as a new loan word, so that we have
   two homonyms *realisieren*.

Loan shifts must also be complex morphological items.
Leaving aside cases of popular etymology (*Volksetymologie*) like
Armbrust, cf. Lat. *arcuballista*, which could be considered here,
we can distinguish two subclasses according to whether the foreign
model is exactly translated component for component: loan translation, or more freely rendered: loan rendition. Further subtypes may be distinguished according to the degree of correspondence
between the word form in the donor and that in the recipient language, but need not detain us here. In all cases, the new word
must be based on a model in a foreign language. Otherwise it
cannot be classified as a borrowing (I leave aside questions of
intralingual borrowing). The substitute words coined by purists
to replace German foreignisms (here the term is apposite) are not
borrowings, as the substitution process takes place within the
German language alone. That the purists did not regard foreignisms as part of the German language need not confuse us here.

A further category remains: loan creation, where the form of
the replacement coinage is quite independent of the foreign model.

In agreement with Höfler, Bäcker and others, I would exclude loan creation from the classes of lexical borrowing. For one thing, the indissoluable unity of form and content of the linguistic sign is not maintained; for another, the loan creations known to me are replacements or puristic substitutes for German foreignisms and thus arise in a monolingual situation. This is clear from Betz's example *Mundart* for *Dialekt*.

The cases I have here excluded from the classes of lexical borrowing are nonetheless relevant to the wider question of foreign influence, and to the etymological structure of German, as they are part and parcel of the history of foreignisms in German. Which brings us back to the foreignisms. Now that consideration of loan substitution has alerted us to questions of the origin of word content or meaning, we must look again at the tacit assumption that the meanings of foreignisms are borrowed too. This is by no means always the case, as the following examples illustrate: *rasant* in the senses 'sehr schnell; dynamisch, stürmisch; schnittig, aufreizend; rassig' is semantically quite independent of the French etymon *rasant* (which incidentally means just the opposite!); *Raffinement* and *Raffinerie* for 'Durchtriebenheit' have no equivalent in the original donor language French; *Transparent* for 'Spruchband' is a purely German semantic development; the German verb *starten* has a different semantic range from its English etymon *start*; and so on and so forth. Of the dictionaries of foreignisms, only the last volumes of Schulz/Basler attempt to distinguish systematically between borrowed and non-borrowed, i.e. native, meanings. The need to etymologise individual word meanings and not to content oneself with a description of the origin of a word form (and its original meaning) is a claim that must clearly be made of etymology in general, not just with regard to foreign influence. So much, then, for word content.

Let me try and summarise my criticism of the traditional view of the etymological structure of German vocabulary in the light of foreign influence in one sentence: Not only can it be demonstrated, as above, that the categories alien or denizen, hybrid and native are at best one-sided, misleading and unfounded, but it can also be shown that the dichotomy between foreignisms and German words is equally untenable, in that many foreignisms, namely the majority of the loan coinages, are really natives rather than aliens, and many 'German' words turn out to be semantic foreignisms. It is time, I conclude, for a new look.

The following diagram represents the outline of a different scheme of things designed to take into account the criticisms I have made of the traditional view. I submit it for discussion without further commentary:

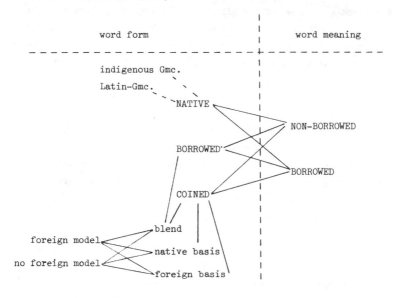

Allow me to conclude with a few general remarks. In re-examining the traditional view of the etymological structure of German vocabulary in the light of foreign influence, I have naturally enough concentrated on that influence and tried to make out a strong case for its importance in the past, at present and for the future. There is, of course, another side to things, the native one of Germanic origin. It should not be forgotten, for example, that the central verbal structures of German are native to the core, that verbal roots of Germanic origin form the basis of the central system of German derivational morphology, and that the common words at the centre of German vocabulary are predominantly natives. But German is more than Basic German. And as we move from the common centre outwards to formal written and literary usage and on to academic and scientific German, foreign influence · progressively increases. In my view, this foreign element has until recently been left too much to the attention of purists and been either ignored or treated as non-German by German linguists. It is time for historical, diachronic lexicology to provide a more adequate description of the etymological structure of German vocabulary. As an end in itself, and as a means to a wider end. It is clear from the constant discussion in the press and from the continued boom on the market for dictionaries of foreignisms that foreignisms are a problem for many, if not most, German speakers. That this continues to be the case suggests that previous approaches to the problem, such as general exhortations to be German and use 'German' words in the apparent belief that they are somehow inherently better and more comprehensible, censure of the use of foreignisms in school and the tradition of separate lexicological and lexicographical treatment, need revision. Perhaps knowledge of the true extent of foreign influence on the formal and semantic structure of German could help relativise the obsessive preoccupation with foreignisms alone, promote a more factual discussion on them in connection with other types of lexical borrowing and lead to more tolerance in the face of the current influx of anglicisms? Perhaps the systematic teaching of word formation elements and patterns in schools could help make more foreignisms, especially more Latinisms, more transparent to more Germans, and perhaps this in turn would help make them more comprehensible? The list of possibilities could be continued. But I hope it is clear enough already that an academic pre-occupation with foreign lexical influence on German has some significance outside the ivory tower.

Notes

1   The spoken text has been retained virtually unchanged.   Foot-
    notes and references have been kept to a bare minimum.

2   Lasswell, H.D. (1964) 'The Structure and Function of
    Communication in Society', *The Communication of Ideas.
    A Series of Addresses*, ed. L. Bryson, New York/London.   I
    thank Wolfgang Mentrup for this reference.

3   The terminology is adapted from James Murray, who in the
    General Explanations to the OED (p. xxix) distinguishes
    between naturals, denizens, aliens and casuals.

4   Augst, G. (1977) 'Fremdwort - fremdes Wort', *Sprachnorm
    und Sprachwandel.   Vier Projekte zu diachroner Sprach-
    betrachtung*, Wiesbaden, Athenaion, 61-123, here 67-68.

5   Link, E. (1983) 'Fremdwörter - der Deutschen liebste
    schwere Wörter?' *Deutsche Sprache* 47-77, here 58-59.

6   Cf. the contribution by Charles Russ in this volume.

7   *Deutsche Wortbildung.   Typen und Tendenzen in der Gegen-
    wartssprache*, Vol. 1-3, Düsseldorf, Schwann 1973-78.

8   Sonдеregger, S. (1979) *Grundzüge deutscher Sprachgeschichte.
    Diachronie des Sprachsystems*, Vol. 1, Berlin/New York,
    de Gruyter.

9   Polenz, P. von (1967) 'Fremdwort und Lehnwort sprachwissen-
    schaftlich betrachtet', *Muttersprache* 77: 65-80.

10 Munske, H.H. (1980) 'Germanische Sprachen und deutsche
    Gesamtsprache', *Lexikon der Germanistischen Linguistik*,
    2nd ed., Tübingen, Niemeyer, 661-672.

11 For a useful summary cf. Betz, W. (1974) 'Lehnwörter und
    Lehnprägungen im Vor- und Frühdeutschen', *Deutsche Wort-
    geschichte*, 3rd ed., Berlin/New York, de Gruyter, 135-163.

12 Bäcker, N. (1975) *Probleme des inneren Lehnguts dargestell
    an den Anglizismen der französischen Sportsprache*, Tübinge
    Narr.

THE FOREIGN ELEMENT IN GERMAN DERIVATIONAL MORPHOLOGY:
THE ADJECTIVAL SUFFIXES

Charles V.J. Russ
(University of York)

    I should like to begin my paper by drawing your attention to
a quotation by that little known linguist Michel Mephrom.

> Die tendenzielle Argumentation vis-à-vis den regulären
> bzw. produktiven Techniken der kontroversen Konstitu-
> ierung der morphologischen Subkomponente realisieren in
> eine superkommunikative und ultrakategoriale Regularität
> der Derivationsstruktur.

In this hour after lunch you may wish to consider at length,
possibly with eyes closed, what that weighty sentence may mean.
That option is unfortunately not open to me so I shall take
another road and examine some of the words themselves, some of
which are complex forms, that is they can be divided into smaller
parts which in turn are used again to build other complex words.
For instance in *produkt/iv*, the first part occurs on its own and
in *Produktion*, with *z* for *kt* in *produzieren* and *Produzent*, while
the whole word occurs in *Produktiv/ität*. The smaller part *-iv*
occurs in other forms such as *impulsiv, qualitativ, objektiv,
attributiv*. Linguists have used the term morpheme for such units
of language smaller than the word. Despite the vagaries and un-
certainties of definition, the term morpheme is still alive and
used to mean a 'minimal distinctive unit of grammar' (Crystal:
1980 : 231). Bloomfield (1935 : 160) made the useful distinction
between a free form such as *Produkt* or *Impuls* and a bound form
such as *-iv*. I wish to examine some of the bound forms of the
derivational morphology of German which are of non-native origin.
I propose to look at what derivational morphology is, review some
of the research carried out into language contact at this level
and then to trace in broad outlines the effect such borrowings
have had during the history of German. To illustrate this I shall
use adjectival suffixes.

The line between inflectional and derivational morphology is
intuitively present and yet criteria for separating the two areas
give different results (Bauer 1983 : 29). .The most telling criterion is that of productivity. Inflectional morphemes and processes apply to almost all forms, e.g. the second person sing.
present tense morpheme *-(e)st* applies to almost all verbs. According to Chomsky derivational morphemes and processes are 'typically
sporadic and only quasi-productive' (1965 : 184). Thus of the
three morphemes *-nis, -heit* and *-"e* used to form abstract nouns
from adjectives or verb stems we get *Finsternis, Blindheit, Träg-
heit, Stille, Länge* not **Finsterheit, *Blindnis, *Trägnis,*Still-
heit* and**Längheit*. This semi-productivity results as a necessity
from the greater number of derivational morphemes compared with
inflectional ones. Wellman (1975b) deals with forty noun suffixes
and Kühnhold et al. (1978) deal with eighteen adjectival suffixes.
The sentence we started with contains the following derivational
suffixes: *-(i)ell, -ation, -isieren, -iv, -ial* and *-ität* and the
prefixes *ultra-, super-, sub-*. Affixes with the same or similar
written form and meaning occur in other languages and this similarity we do not want to ascribe to their being part of the original
vocabulary of a proto-language but due to later contact between
German and other languages. These foreign affixes have received
differing treatments by linguists. Henzen (1965) and Wilmanns
(1899) deal with them very briefly with no real mention of when
they were borrowed. Seiler (1913-24) is much more detailed,
stressing the distinction between Latin and French suffixes and
giving some dating of words containing them. Rosenfeld (1974)
gives a well documented account of those suffixes borrowed during
the humanist period. The real doyen of borrowing foreign suffixes is without doubt Öhmann who in detailed articles has covered
most of the foreign suffixes, but largely centring on noun suffixes and the struggle between French and Latin suffixes, e.g.
-ös and *-os* (1937). At the Institut für deutsche Sprache a
project is under way entitled 'Synchrone und diachrone Untersuchungen zur Wortbildungen mit entlehnten Elementen im Deutschen
(Lehnwortbildung)' which will examine this subject in detail.

The first task of our investigation is to ascertain what
counts as a foreign suffix. What criteria can be applied and
what results do they yield? Phonetically the main characteristic
of foreign suffixes is that they receive full stress: *tendenziéll,
regulär, produktív*. Some exceptions to this final stressing of
foreign suffixes are noted in Duden Fremdwörterbuch (1974 : 16):

> Außerdem werden die üblicherweise endungsbetonten fremd-
> sprachlichen Wörter oftmals auch auf der ersten Silbe
> betont wenn sie im Affekt gesprochen werden oder wenn sie
> wegen ihrer sachlichen Wichtigkeit besonders hervorge-
> hoben oder auch in Gegensatz zu anderen gestellt werden
> sollen.

A consequence of the foreign suffixes being stressed is that a
large number of vowels occurs: *produktív, Natúr, religiös, kuriós,
forméll, formál*. The native suffixes, being largely unstressed,
or semi-stressed, show a much reduced range, chiefly [-I-] and
[-ə-].

At other levels of linguistic analysis foreign suffixes
behave much the same as native ones. The adjectives compare and
decline with no problems. The only exceptions are colour terms
such as *rosa, orange, beige* etc. The morphemes which combine
with them are both bound stems, e.g. *Information, informieren,
informativ*, and free roots, *produktiv* from *Produkt*.

Semantically the range of meanings given to the suffixes
varies with both native and foreign ones. Kühnhold et al (1978)
ascribe twenty-five meanings or functions to the native suffix *-ig*
and fourteen meanings or functions to the foreign suffix *-iv*. As
in the case of other loans the main traditional identification of
them is through their presence in another language, thus: German
produktiv, English *productive*, French *productif*. In this paper
the criterion of form has been used to identify foreign suffixes
but using familiarity of meaning, as Alan Kirkness suggests, might
lead to different results, whereby for example *Information* by dint
of its frequent use might not be classed 'foreign'. Suffixes,
however, are never borrowed initially per se, but only loan words
containing the suffixes.

> Es werden nur ganze Wörter entlehnt, niemals Ableitungs-
> und Flexionssuffixe. Wird aber eine größere Anzahl
> von Wörtern entlehnt, die das gleiche Suffix enthalten, so
> schließe sich dieselben ebensogut zu einer Gruppe zu-
> sammen wie einheimische Wörter mit dem gleichen Suffix,
> und eine solche Gruppe kann dann auch produktiv werden.
> (Paul 1920 : 399)

The speakers of the receiving language will not normally be
aware of the morphological divisions of a word that has been
borrowed.   When other words from the same word family are borrowed, then a pattern starts to emerge, a word family is formed
whose members can be morphologically analysed into stem + affix.
In this study I shall be primarily concerned with such complex
lexical items which are analysable in German into stem plus suffix,
in other words motivated or transparent forms.   Thus although
there are several adjectives in NHG which end in *-id*: *arid, gravid,*
hybrid, invalid, livid, liquid, morbid, perfid, rapid, rigid,
splendid, solid, stupid, torpid,   the stem, i.e. what remains of
the word after the *-id* has been removed, e.g. *ar-, hybr-, sol-* etc.
does not occur elsewhere either on its own or attached to another
morpheme.   Adjectives in *-id* will thus be regarded as unanalysable
units.   (There are however three adjectives where *-id* seems to
be isolable: *negrid* from *Neger* and *europäid, europid* from *Europa.*)
Thus we will not consider *-id* to be part of the German derivation
morphology nor *-an, -än* nor *-at*.   We will be concerned solely
with productive or living foreign suffixes.   But what does it
mean to say that a suffix is productive or living?   One recent
definition is by L. Bauer (1983 : 100)

> ... a morphological process can be said to be more or
> less productive according to the number of new words
> which it is used to form.

Thus among native nominal suffixes the feminine forming *-in* is the
most productive accounting for 97% of formations, whereas the suffixes *-euse, -ine, -esse* and *-sche* which have a similar meaning
make up the other 3% (Wellmann 1975 : 109-118).   With regard to
the productivity of foreign suffixes the principle is often stated
that a foreign suffix becomes productive when it is combined with
a native base, e.g. *Druckerei, Stellage.*

If the new suffix appears in conjunction with native
stems, the suffixation process has become productive and
a new suffix has been added to the borrowing language.
(Jeffers and Lehiste 1979 : 152)

This is the optimum of the productivity and integration of a loan
suffix into the derivational word formation system of a language.
Combination with native stems to form 'hybrid' forms does not
always occur however. The suffix *-iv* never combines with native
bases and yet is clearly productive in modern German (Kühnhold et
al. 1978 : 379f). The question of productivity seems straight-
forward enough when posed diachronically. Given sufficient evidence it will soon be clear whether over the course of time new
words will have been created. We will use Bauer's definition
but interpret it historically.

The area that I intend to study as exemplification is that
of the adjectival suffixes *-abel/-ibel, -al/-ell, -ant/-ent,
-ar/-är, -iv* and *-os/-ös*. I used the material provided by Mater
(1965) and Kühnhold et al. (1978) to provide a basic corpus of
adjectives with these suffixes. I then tried to determine when
they were first used and thus to present a profile of productivity
over the centuries. Adjectives were chosen because they form a
smaller percentage of borrowings, nouns being most numerous, followed by verbs, and were thus eminently manageable. Secondly it
turned out that in most cases nouns especially and/or verbs with
the same base had been borrowed earlier. There were thus clear
patterns in existence. The different forms of the suffixes result from the different language of origin, thus *-ant, -al, -ar*
and *-os* are from the Latin endings while *-ell, -ent, -är* and *-ös*
are from French endings. The *-abel/-ibel* variation does not
reflect this distinction of origin. Kühnhold et al. (1978 : 36-40)
describe the variations synchronically. In fourteen cases there
is a semantic opposition between forms in *-al* and *-ell* (Kühnhold
et al. 1978 : 38), e.g. *formal* vs. *formell*. Only a certain proportion of the corpus could be dated. Schulz/Basler shows a great
unevenness of cover and detail between the first two volumes and
the later ones which contain much more information. Similarly the

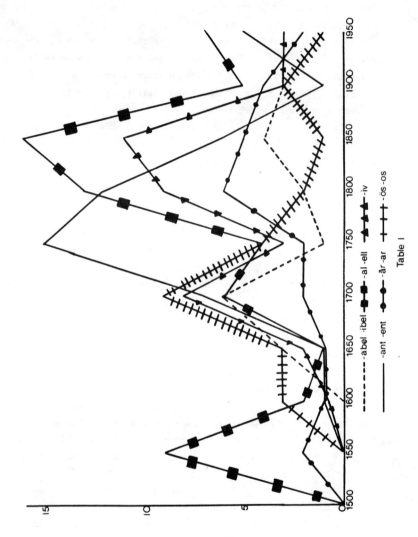

Table I

revised *Grimm: Deutsches Wörterbuch* is excellent but only as far
as it has proceeded: *A - Ackerteil* by the Berlin group and *D -
drücken* by the Göttingen group.   Given these shortcomings a fairly
clear picture emerged. which is illustrated by Table 1.   The hori-
zontal axis shows the dates from 1500 to 1950 divided into fifty
year stretches.   The vertical axis shows the number of forms recorded.   The intersections of the two axes show the number of new
forms at a particular half century.

Before examining the results in detail two preliminary remarks
must be made.

    1. The low figures for 1900-1950 represent the lack of
    documentation for the modern period.   Schulz/Basler had
    only proceeded to P by 1942 and the revision of *Grimms
    Deutsche Wörterbuch* only deals with *A-Ack* and *D-drücken*.
    2. The lack of forms between 1500-1550 probably represents
    a real lack of foreign adjectives.   In fact only adjectives
    in *-al/-ell* and *-är/-ar* are recorded then.
Adjectives tend to be borrowed less frequently than nouns.   Kettmann (1978 : 409) shows borrowed adjectives only accounting for
between 1% and 8.1% in the early sixteenth century according to
author and stylistic level whereas nouns range from 85-100%.

During the period 1649 to 1735 Brunt (1983 : 96) has only
15.2% adjectival borrowings as against 16.7% for verbs and a massive 63.1% for nouns.

The table shows a gradual accretion of borrowed adjectives
with peaks in the eighteenth and nineteenth centuries.

The suffix *-abel/-ibel* starts to occur at the beginning of
the seventeenth century with a peak between 1650 and 1700.

The suffix *-ant/-ent* starts to occur around 1550 and reaches
its peak between 1700 and 1750.

The suffix *-al/-ell* starts to occur about 1500, climbs steeply
to 1550, slumps after that but peaks between 1800 and 1850.

The suffix *-är/-ar* starts after 1500 and progresses steadily
throughout, peaking between 1750 and 1800.

The suffix *-iv* starts to occur about 1550 and is infrequent until after 1650 when it rises, falls slightly around 1750 and then rises steadily to a peak around 1850.

The suffix *-ös/-os* starts to occur after 1550, climbing steadily to its peak around 1700 after which it drops to rise again slightly after 1850.

The peaks between 1700 and 1850 are no doubt due to the growth of German for scientific and technical purposes. They reflect the creation of a technical register for German (Keller 1978 : 485f). ·Only a relatively small number of adjectives could be dated. By far the larger part were not recorded in any dictionary. The following figures make that clear:

	dated	undated
-abel/-ibel	19	100
-ant/-ent	41	62
-al/-ell	–	187
-är/-ar	25	66
-iv	36	91
-ös/-os	27	62
	210(27%)	568(73%)

Thus only 27% of the total adjectives could be dated. The conclusion one could draw from this is that most, if not all, the undated forms are from the nineteenth and twentieth centuries and from technical registers. They form such a large percentage that their occurrence has simply been hitherto underrated and they have been relegated to *Fremdwörterbücher*. Articulatory phonetics gained great fame in the nineteenth century and many of the adjectives describing place and manner of articulation are undated: *velar, uvular; dorsal, labial, nasal, palatal.* Other adjectives are of limited occurrence in technical languages: *bazillär, fibrillär, retikular, bifilar; ferruginös, fibrös, kankrös, gangränös, skabrös.*

Two suffixes which are not covered by the historical studies are *-esk* and *-oid.* Mater (1965 : 285) only gives *balladesk,* *chevaleresk* as transparent forms, but Kühnhold (1978 : 338f.) gives twenty-eight examples showing how *-esk* is productive, but mainly with the names of well known literary figures *kafkaesk.* Mater (1965 : 11) only gives *negroid, paranoid* and *schizoid* as examples of adjectives with *-oid* but Kühnhold (1978 : 330f.) cites thirty-eight cases mostly from technical language of medicine or designation of a person. Thus 'new' adjectival patterns are still becoming productive. Wellmann (1975a) deals with these two suffixes and points to the differences in their sociolinguistic distribution. The suffixes *-esk* and *-oid* are only productive in the use of journalists, writers and literary scholars.

The adjectival suffixes that I have dealt with came from Latin and/or French into German and one also to be found in English, again owing to borrowing from these two languages. If we look at the list of adjectives in *-iv* we can see that many if not most of them have corresponding forms in French and English. They thus belong to the realm of what Braun (1979 : 131) has called *Internationalismen* which are due, among other things, to mutual borrowing between English, French and German. Through these internationalisms there is a convergence of certain areas of the vocabulary, notably politics, science, academic disciplines, medicine, so that apart from the grammar a text from these registers in each language can look very similar.

In this conference we shall be considering various aspects of the influence of other languages on German and of German on English and it is as well at the beginning to set these trends in a European context. A study of some adjectival suffixes in German has, I hope, shown a way we can move in that direction.

References

L. Bauer (1983) *English Word-formation.* C.U.P.

L. Bloomfield (1935) *Language.* London.

P. Braun (1979) *Tendenzen in der deutschen Gegenwartssprache.* Kohlhammer: Stuttgart. Urban TB 297.

R.J. Brunt (1983) *The Influence of the French Language on the German Vocabulary (1649-1735).* De Gruyter: Berlin.

N. Chomsky (1965) *Aspects of the theory of syntax.* MIT Press: Cambridge, Mass.

D. Crystal (1980) *A first dictionary of linguistics and phonetics.* André Deutsch: London.

Duden Fremdwörterbuch (1974) *Der Duden Band 5.* 3rd edition. Mannheim: Bibliographisches Institut.

W. Henzen (1965) *Deutsche Wortbildung.* Niemeyer: Tübingen.

R.J. Jeffers and I. Lehiste (1979) *Principles and methods for historical linguistics.* MIT Press: Cambridge, Mass.

W.J. Jones (1976) *A Lexicon of French Borrowings in the German Vocabulary (1575-1648).* De Gruyter: Berlin.

R.E. Keller (1978) *The German language.* Faber and Faber: London.

G. Kettmann (1978) 'Zum Fremdwortgebrauch', in: *Zur Literatursprache im Zeitalter der frühbürgerlichen Revolution.* Akademie: Berlin, 341-439.

I. Kühnhold, O. Putzer, H. Wellmann (1978) *Deutsche Wortbildung 3. Das Adjektiv.* Schwann: Düsseldorf.

E. Mater (1965) *Rückläufiges Wörterbuch.* Leipzig.

E. Öhmann (1937) 'Über einige frz. Suffixe im Deutschen', *Neuphilologische Mitteilungen* 38, 305-321.

H. Paul (1920) *Prinzipien der Sprachgeschichte.* Halle.

H.-Fr. Rosenfeld (1974-8) 'Humanistische Strömungen', in: F. Maurer, H. Rupp ed. *Deutsche Wortgeschichte* 3rd ed. De Gruyter: Berlin.

H. Schulz *Deutsches Fremdwörterbuch.* Vol. 1 (A-K) 1913, II, continued by O. Basler, (L-P), 1942, III, continued by IdS (Q-R) 1977, IV S 1977-8, V T 1979-80, VI U-V, 1981.

F. Seiler (1913[2]-1924) *Die Entwicklung der deutschen Kultur im Spiegel des deutschen Lehnworts.* 8 vols. (3 Teil)

H. Wellmann (1975a) 'Fremdwörter des Lexikons oder systemgebundene Ableitungen? über die Integration der Adjektive auf -esk (und -oid)', *Sprachsystem und Sprachgebrauch. Festschrift für Hugo Moser. Teil 2.* Schwann: Düsseldorf, 409-431.

H. Wellmann (1975b) *Deutsche Wortbildung 2. Das Substantiv.* Schwann: Düsseldorf.

W. Wilmanns (1899) *Deutsche Grammatik.* Band 2. *Abteilung: Wortbildung.* Strasbourg.

DATED ADJECTIVES

in -abel/-ibel

räsonnabel	1616
tolerabel	1616
miserabel	1642
horribel	1652
kapabel	1661
sensibel	1662
traktabel	1674
abominabel	1695
disputabel	1696
detestabel	1723
respektabel	1776
transportabel	1787
reduzibel	19th c
komfortabel	1805
demonstrabel	1807
trätabel	1842
rentabel	1858
diskutabel	1868
suggestibel	1891

in -ant/-ent

permanent	1581	rasant	1741
solvent	1650	galant	1746
suffisant	1633	frappant	1758
korpulent	1656	tolerant	1761
insolent	1659	elegant	1765
penetrant	1677	stringent	1765
pikant	1682	transparent	1779
scharmant	1688	renitent	1766
relevant	1689	eminent	1788
prägnant	1698	imposant	1788
eklatant	1707	konsequent	1788
opulent	1708	dezent	1790
evident	1708	patent	1790
impertinent	1714	fulminant	1796
meschant	1714	latent	1800
extravagant	1714	intelligent	1801
exorbitant	1718	ambulant	1801
nonchalant	1719	frequent	1803
medisant	1727	genant	1829
konstant	1727	markant	1835
mokant	1728	kulant	1855
kompetent	1731	prominent	1908
interessant	1740	resistent	1958

in -al/-ell

finanziell	16th c	formal	1793
notariell	1516	offizinell	1795
triumphal	1522	rationell	1798
synodal	1522	ideell	1800
sakramental	1526	kolossal	1800
proportional	1527	kolonial	1800
konfessional	1530	rituell	1801
trivial	1535	normal	1806
radikal	1537	semestral	1809
national	1571	nominell	1813
total	1574	traditionell	1823
real	1607	ministerial	1828
territorial	1661	industriell	1831
fatal	1664	spiral	1832
fundamental	1671	tangentiell	1836
naturell	1683	international	1838
spirituell	1689	sensationell	1839
reell	1694	oppositionell	1848
pastell	1712	phänomenal	1850
aktuell	1727	dental	1861
formell	1731	experimentell	1871
sensuell	1765	maximal	1871
originell	1766	redaktionell	1898
sentimental	1769	differentiell	1900
diagonal	1774	direktorial	1911
sexuell	1783	regional	1918
rustikal	1784	dimensional	1922
temporell	1784	tonal	1925
sexual	1787	strukturell	1929
offiziell	1792	saisonal	1937
pastoral	1792		

in -är/-ar

konträr	1525
sakulär	1530
ordinär	1566
singulär	1642
familiär	1657
polar	18th c
solitär	1703
lapidar	1778
sekundär	1781
pekuniär	1788
prekär	1789
temporär	1789
revolutionär	1797
stationär	1810
subsidiär	1826
doktrinär	1830
primär	1838
reaktionär	1842
sedimentär	1851
rudimentär	1871
quartär	1875
sanitär	1879
parasitär	1929
totalitär	1937

in -iv

offensiv	1590	representativ	1798
possessiv	17th c	suggestiv	1809
effektiv	1618	qualitativ	1819
massiv	1652	exklusiv	1831
positiv	1652	konservativ	1834
aktiv	1680	repressiv	1834
suspensiv	1695	quantitativ	1835
präsumtiv	18th c	rezeptiv	1840
spekulativ	1701	definitiv	1840
vegetativ	1719	subversiv	1843
relativ	1757	instinktiv	1845
objektiv	1761	regressiv	1878
intensiv	1767	impulsiv	1883
negativ	1769	ostentativ	1899
instruktiv	1775	reflexiv	19th c
progressiv	1787	reaktiv	1925
regulativ	1788	ultimativ	1925
passiv	1796	selektiv	1933

in -ös/-os

skrupulös	1569
skandalös	1575
rigoros	1592
famos	1603
monströs	1608
kurios	1627
ominös	1661
furios	1665
generös	1665
ingeniös	1677
ruinös	1678
seriös	1681
luxuriös	1681
kapriziös	1688
respektuös	1688
mysteriös	18th c
gratiös	1700
spiritös	1732
sentenziös	1739
irreligiös	1776
grandios	1781
serös	1809
tendentiös	1857
strapaziös	1870
desaströs	1876
schikanös	1930

ANMERKUNGEN ZUR ANGLIZISMUSFORSCHUNG

Gerhard Stickel
(Institut für deutsche Sprache)

Was im folgenden dargelegt werden soll, sind vor allem etwas
persönlich gefärbte impressionistische Beobachtungen und Überlegungen zur Erforschung der Anglizismen in der deutschen Gegenwartssprache. Es sind Anmerkungen und Nachbemerkungen zu den
theoretisch orientierten Ausführungen meines Institutskollegen
Kirkness. Erst diese Tagung und ihr Thema wurden für mich zum
Anlaß, mich etwas eingehender mit den Ergebnissen der Anglizismusforschung zu befassen. Mir wurde dabei rasch klar, daß das Feld
der Beobachtung und Analyse der Anglizismen im heutigen Deutsch
ganz vorzüglich beackert und bestellt ist, und zwar vor allem
von deutschsprachigen Anglisten und einigen englischsprachigen
Germanisten. Den Kennern der Szene ist zweifellos bekannt, daß
Galinsky (1972), Carstensen (1965), Fink (1970), Viereck (1980)
und ihre Schüler and Mitarbeiter durchweg Anglisten sind oder
anglistisch ausgebildet sind. Hinzu kommen die englischsprachigen
Germanisten, die sich als 'Anglizisten' betätigen, wie Clyne
(1973), Duckworth (1970) und Stanforth (1968).

Die muttersprachliche Germanistik hat sich in neuerer Zeit
nicht speziell mit Anglizismen befaßt. Von deutschen Germanisten
wie Werner Betz (1945) und Peter von Polenz (1967) stammen jedoch
einige grundlegende Arbeiten zur Fremd- und Lehnwortproblematik.
Ihnen ist zu verdanken, daß die Wörter und Endungen im Deutschen,
die erkennbare morphologische Elemente aus dem Englischen enthalten oder die in ihrer syntagmatischen Struktur und/oder in
ihrer Bedeutung auf englische Vorbilder schließen lassen, inzwischen wiederholt typenmäßig analysiert und klassifiziert worden
sind, so wie auch Alan Kirkness vorgegangen ist.

Zur Strukturbeschreibung der in reicher Zahl gesammelten
Ausdrücke kann ein Anglizismusneuling nicht viel Neues beitragen.
Bis aber die über 60.000 Belege von Broder Carstensen in Paderborn
alle analysiert und zu einem umfassenden Wörterbuch der

Anglizismen verarbeitet sind, wird freilich noch einige Zeit vergehen. Ich komme auf dieses Vorhaben später noch einmal zurück.

Forschungslücken scheinen mir in zwei anderen Bereichen zu bestehen, in denen sich noch nicht so viele Kollegen tummeln und in denen, soweit ich sehe, noch viel Arbeit zu leisten ist. Ich meine:

- die Erforschung der Einstellungen zum Gebrauch von Anglizismen und

- die Erforschung der Abnutzungsrate oder positiv: der relativen Beständigkeit von Anglizismen im deutschen Wortschatz.

Zunächst zur Einstellungsforschung

In seinem detaillierten Bericht über die neuere Anglizismusforschung (W. Viereck 1980), werden zwar einige Arbeiten referiert, in denen auch die *Bewertung* des Gebrauchs von Anglizismen behandelt wurde, dies aber nur nebenbei. Soweit ich die referierten Arbeiten und Vierecks eigene Untersuchungen überprüft habe, ergab sich, daß die Hauptfragen aller größeren Arbeiten auf die Verständlichkeit und Gebrauchsüblichkeit von jeweils vorgegebenen ausgewählten Ausdrücken gerichtet waren. Zu den wenigen Arbeiten, in denen auf die Motive für den Gebrauch von Anglizismen explizit eingegangen wird, gehört die von Michael G. Clyne (1973). In der Annahme, daß Hauptquellen für die Verbreitung von Anglizismen die Texte der Medien und der Werbung sind, befragte Clyne Vertreter von Werbeangenturen, Zeitungen, Rundfunk- und Fernsehsendern nach ihren Kriterien für den Gebrauch von Anglizismen. Die Antworten waren jedoch nicht besonders ergiebig, weil die meisten Redakteure und Werbeleute vorgaben, nur solche englischen Wörter zu benutzen, die ohnehin schon ins 'Allgemeingut' eingegangen seien. Clyne gibt nicht an, wie er seine Informanten befragt hat. Es wäre sicher lohnend, die Befragung der Werbefachleute zu wiederholen, und zwar mit präzis vorbereitetem Fragekatalog. Jeder, der auch nur einen flüchtigen Eindruck von der

Sprache der Werbung für Waschmittel, Kosmetik- und Textilprodukte
in den deutschsprachigen Ländern gewonnen hat, weiß, daß Michael
Clyne von den Werbeagenturen nicht die Wahrheit erfahren hat.
Das früher für die Anglizismenforschung ergiebige Feld der Werbung
für Tabakprodukte gibt inzwischen nicht mehr viel her, weil die
Werbung stark eingeschränkt worden ist.

Wichtiger als die Untersuchung der Motive für die aktive
Benutzung von Anglizismen ist die Ermittlung der Einstellungen
auf der Seite der Hörer und Leser. Hierzu gibt es bisher lediglich einige kleinere Studien und eine Reihe von Einzelbeobacht-
ungen und Überlegungen in größeren Arbeiten über Anglizismen, etwa
denen von Carstensen (1965) und Fink (1970). Was die Methoden
zur Ermittlung der Einstellung angeht, sind zwei Verfahren vor-
herrschend: Entweder gibt der Linguist seine persönliche Einschät-
zung wieder, die sich teilweise auf informelle Gespräche mit
anderen Textkonsumenten stützt, oder es werden ausgewählte
Probanden gezielt zu Wortlisten befragt, z.B.: 'Wer würde Ihrer
Meinung nach das Wort *Disengagement* verwenden?' oder 'Verwenden
Sie dieses Wort selbst?'.

Das erste Verfahren, das im Grunde ja keine empirische
Methode ist, liegt den Einschätzungen zugrunde, die mehrere Autoren
zu Einstellungsbewertungen abgeben. Das Verfahren der gezielten
Befragung wurde u.a. von Viereck/Viereck/Winter (1975) und
Viereck (1980) in Österreich angewandt. Nur ging es dabei, wie
gesagt, nicht primär um die Erforschung von Einstellungen.

Überhaupt nicht systematisch genutzt hat die bisherige
Anglizismusforschung eine sehr naheliegende Quelle für die Ermittlung von Einstellungen: nämlich Sprachanfragen an Institutionen
und sprachkritische Glossen und Leserbriefe in Zeitungen und
Zeitschriften. Solche Texte haben den Vorteil, daß sie nicht in
einer formellen Befragungssituation entstehen, sondern von den
Verfassern freiwillig angeboten werden. Sie enthalten zumeist
auch Werturteile, die auf die Einstellung der Verfasser schließen
lassen. Sprachanfragen, Leserbriefe und Sprachglossen als
Quellen für die Einstellungsforschung zu verwenden, ist nicht

unproblematisch. Die Frage nach der Repräsentativität bleibt
dabei ohne statistisch befriedigende Antwort. Es gibt etwa den
Typ des notorischen Leserbriefschreibers, der an allem und jedem
Anstoß nimmt. Sprachsoziologisch wichtige Merkmale wie Ausbil-
dung, Beruf, Alter, Geschlecht, Fremdsprachenkenntnisse usw. sind
aus Leserbriefen nur zum Teil oder gar nicht zu entnehmen. Dies
gilt auch für viele Sprachanfragen und fast alle Sprachglossen,
die von Zeitungsredakteuren geschrieben werden.

Abgesehen von den Querulanten läßt sich aber annehmen, daß
derartige Texte vor allem von sprachlich besonders empfindsamen
bzw. empfindlichen Mitbürgern geschrieben werden und damit symp-
tomatisch für die Spracheinstellung vieler anderer stehen, die
lediglich zurückhaltender sind oder über sprachliche Fragen
weniger gründlich nachdenken.

Um einen ersten Eindruck zu gewinnen, ob sich die Auswertung
solcher Quellen überhaupt lohnen würde, habe ich mir in den
letzten Tagen die Sprachanfragen, die an unser Institut gerichtet
wurden, und die einschlägigen Sprachglossen und Leserbriefe, die
bei uns gesammelt worden sind, etwas näher angesehen. Aus Zeit-
gründen mußte ich mich auf Texte aus den letzten Jahren be-
schränken, und zwar vornehmlich solche, die sich auf Fremdwörter,
insbesondere Anglizismen beziehen.

Zunächst eine Bemerkung zu den Sprachanfragen und -beschwerden.
Unter den vielen Anfragen zu ganz unterschiedlichen sprachlichen
Problemen finden sich auch immer wieder Briefe, in denen unser
Institut aufgefordert wird, etwas gegen den Verfall der deutschen
Sprache zu tun, und zwar vor allem gegen die Flut von Anglizismen
vorzugehen, um damit für einen besseren und verständlicheren
Sprachgebrauch zu sorgen. Die meist pauschale Klage, daß Texte
und mündliche Äußerungen wegen des Gebrauchs von Fremdwörtern
schwer verständlich sind, findet sich in mehreren dieser Briefe.
Auf weitere Motive für negative Einstellungen zu Anglizismen oder
Fremdwörtern generell gehe ich gleich noch ein.

. Da mich Anglizismen wenigstens bis vor kurzem nicht sonder-
lich gestört haben - mich stört allenfalls der Anglizismusgebrauch

einzelner Menschen oder in bestimmten Textsorten -, habe ich solche
puristischen Aufforderungen nie so ganz ernst genommen. Und das
gilt auch für meine Mannheimer Kollegen, die ähnlich wie ich auf
derartige Eingaben meist geantwortet haben, unser Institut sei
eine reine Forschungseinrichtung ohne sprachpflegerische Aufgaben,
und im übrigen sei das mit den Fremdwörtern nicht so schlimm;
Wortentlehnungen aus anderen Sprachen habe es im Deutschen immer
schon gegeben. Sprache und Sprachgemeinschaft hätten solche
Einflüsse bisher stets ohne großen Schaden verarbeitet. Diese
Weise, mit den sprachlichen Problemen unserer Mitbürger umzugehen,
war zugegebenermaßen etwas leichtfertig und oberflächlich, letzt-
lich aber, wie ich meine, linguistisch und sprachpolitisch richtig.

Da die Briefe über Fremdwortfragen, die an unser Institut
gerichtet worden sind, eine recht zufällige und zu geringe Auswahl an sprachkritischen Äußerungen über Anglizismen darstellen,
habe ich, wie gesagt, Leserbriefe und Sprachglossen aus Zeitungen
und Zeitschriften hinzugenommen und damit insgesamt eine Art
Mischkorpus aus rund hundert Texten gebildet. Diese Texte
variieren in ihrer Länge zwischen einigen wenigen Sätzen und
mehreren eng beschriebenen Briefseiten. Die Zahl 100 ist deshalb
nur bedingt wichtig.

Zwei Hauptgruppen lassen sich unterscheiden:

1. Die weitaus größere Menge von Texten, in denen der
    Gebrauch von 'Fremdwörtern' (ich benutze diesen
    Ausdruck hier als Zitat) bemängelt wird.

2. Texte, in denen der Gebrauch von Fremdwörtern abge-
    wogen oder sogar positiv beurteilt wird. Zu dieser
    Gruppe zähle ich auch Texte, die lediglich Hinweise
    zum besseren Gebrauch von Wörtern mit fremdsprach-
    lichen Merkmalen geben wollen.

Zur ersten Gruppe gehören bis auf eine Ausnahme alle Briefe
und ein Teil der Sprachglossen. Zur zweiten Gruppe, also den
abgewogenen oder positiven Stellungnahmen gehören die übrigen
Sprachglossen und lediglich ein Leserbrief: Dieser Brief stammt

aus einer Diskussion, die vor einiger Zeit in der Wochenzeit-
schrift 'Die Zeit' zur Fremdwortfrage geführt wurde. Im Unterschied zu allen anderen Briefschreibern meinte der Verfasser, ein
16-jähriger Schüler u.a.:

> Ein Industriestaat wie die Bundesrepublik lebt vom
> *Know-How*, vom internationalen Austausch von Informationen
> jeder Art. Dadurch ist unsere Sprache einer Flut von
> Fremdwörtern ausgesetzt, die unseren Wortschatz erheb-
> lich bereichern. Eine Fremdsprache zu lernen ist
> schwierig und langwierig. Diese schrittweise Annäherung
> der Sprachen durch eingedeutschte Fremdwörter verläuft
> so für den Durchschnittsbürger ohne Sprachtalent ver-
> ständlicher.

Da Leserbriefe jeder Art fast immer eine kritische Stellung-
nahme zu Ereignissen oder Meinungen enthalten (sonst würden
sie nicht geschrieben), erklärt sich dieser positive Leserbrief
in erster Linie aus den in der Zeitung vorausgegangenen negativen
Äußerungen zur Fremdwortfrage.

Zunächst aber zu den vielleicht weniger vernünftigeren, aber
aufschlußreicheren Texten der ersten Gruppe! Ich habe diese
Texte unter drei Fragestellungen geprüft:

   (1) Welche sprachlichen Ausdrücke werden kritisiert?
   (2) Wie wird die negative Bewertung begründet?
   (3) Welche Konsequenzen werden gefordert oder vorgeschlagen?

Schon wegen ihrer unterschiedlichen Länge lassen sich nur in
einem Teil der Texte jeweils Antworten auf alle drei Fragen
finden.

Zu (1): Art der kritisierten Ausdrücke

Wenig ergiebig sind die Texte, in denen ganz pauschal der
Gebrauch von Fremdwörtern, was immer damit alles gemeint ist,
negativ bewertet wird. Verbunden sind damit meist auch nur sehr
allgemeine Begründungen und Änderungsvorschläge.

Interessanter sind die Texte, in denen explizit von 'Anglizismen' oder 'Amerikanismen' die Rede ist und die entsprechende
Beispiele enthalten. Das Phänomen des häufigen Gebrauchs von

Wörtern englischer oder vermeintlich englischer Herkunft wird mehreren Texten als *Engleutsch*, *Deuglisch* oder *Deunglisch* bezeichnet.   Im Unterschied zum *franglais* von Etiemble hat sich demnach im Deutschen noch keine Standardbezeichnung herausgebildet.

Die Wortbeispiele bieten nicht viel Neues.   Soweit ich das im einzelnen überprüfen konnte, sind die meisten der bemängelten Wörter in den bisherigen Arbeiten der Anglizismusforschung beschrieben.   Im Zweifel hat Herr Carstensen sie alle in seiner großen Belegsammlung.   Bemerkenswert ist aber, das einzelne Wörter selbst in meiner kleinen und relativ zufälligen Textauswahl mehrere Male genannt werden: allen voran das immer wieder gescholtene *o.k.*, außerdem *City*, *Ticket*, *Team*, *Teenager*, *Make-up*, *Service*, *Jeans*, *Party* und einige andere ausdrücke, die derart häufig gebraucht werden, daß sie zumindest unter dem Aspekt der Gebräuchlichkeit und Verständlichkeit keinen Anlaß zur Kritik bieten dürften.

Einige der Sprachglossen gehen geordnet vor und nehmen jeweils bestimmte Paradigmen auf's Korn;   z.B. die außerordentlich produktiven Bildungen mit *-center* wie *Kino-Center*, *Buch-Center*, *Foto-Center*, *Fitness-Center* bis hin zum *Sex-Center* (Was das ist, hat der Sprachkritiker leider nicht erklärt).   Besonders die Mischformern, also die Hybridbildungen wie *Freizeit-Dress*, *Blazer-Anzug*, *Klima-Boy*, *Kartoffel-Dressing*, *Korrektur-Fluid*, *Reise-Shop*, die vor allem als Produktnamen und in der Werbesprache häufig sind, werden als Beispiele oder Bildungsmuster in mehreren Texten bemängelt.   Dies gilt auch für morphologisch teilassimilierte Wörter mit einem Stammorphem englischer Herkunft, insbesondere Verben in der Form des 2. Partizips wie *timen/getimed*, *gestreßt*, *gecashed*, *gestylt* und andere.   Ebenfalls bemängelt werden in einigen Texten Ausdrücke, deren Gebrauch vom Englischen beeinflußt ist, die aber analog zu Entlehnungen aus dem Französischen assimiliert sind: allen voran *Frustration* und seine innerdeutschen Abwandlungen *Frust*, *frustrieren*, *frustriert*; außerdem: *Innovation*, *Deklaration*, *Indoktrination*, *Priorität*

und Verben wie *akzeptieren, kontrollieren* und *realisieren,* bei
deren neuerem Gebrauch eigentlich nur eine Bedeutungsentlehnung
vorliegt.

Soviel zur Frage nach der Art der kritisierten Wörter.

Zu (2): Gründe für die Kritik

Die Frage (2) nach den Gründen für die negative Bewertung
von Anglizismen ergibt ein recht buntscheckiges Bild, weil hier
in den einzelnen Texten die vermuteten Gründe für den kritisierten
Gebrauch von Anglizismen in vielfältiger Weise mit der Begründung
der eigenen kritischen Einstellung vermengt wird. Ich will ver-
suchen, diese beiden Begründungsarten etwas zu entwirren:

Zu den Gründen, die für den stets als übertrieben bewerteten
Gebrauch von Anglizismen vermutet werden, gehören vor allem:

- Denkfaulheit. Viele Deutsche seien zu bequem, für neue
  Dinge, Sachverhalte, Begriffe aus dem vorhandenen Wort-
  material geeignete Ausdrücke zu bilden; sie entlehnten
  stattdessen mit der Sache auch das Wort aus dem englischsprachigen Bereich.

- Kritiklose Bewunderung für alles Fremde, früher für alles
  Französische, dann für alles Britische und seit dem Krieg
  für alles Amerikanische; sprachliche Anbiederung beim
  'großen Bruder'.

- Anglizismusgebrauch als Imponiergehabe und zur Ver-
  schleierung, dies besonders in der Werbesprache.

- Druck der Siegermächte, vor allem der USA, im Rahmen
  der sog. 'Umerziehung' nach Kriegsende.

Der letzte Grund wird nur in einem Leserbrief genannt.
Diese Behauptung ist nur deshalb nicht völlig abwegig, als der
vermehrte Englischunterricht in der Bundesrepublik und Österreich auch eine Folge des letzten Krieges ist, wenn auch nur sehr
indirekt. Der Englischunterricht in den Schulen fördert zweifellos den Gebrauch von Anglizismen.

Als Hauptgründe für die negative Bewertung der Anglizismen
im Deutschen werden genannt:

- Durch die denkfaule Übernahme von sprachlichen Elementen
  aus dem Englischen würde die deutsche Sprache Schaden
  leiden, sie würde nicht mehr den neuen Bedürfnissen an-
  gepaßt und damit u.a. nach und nach ihre Literaturfähigkeit
  verlieren.

- Eine Variante dieser Begründung ist: Die Sprache ver-
  armt, weil differenzierte Bezeichnungsmöglichkeiten durch
  Pauschalanglizismen ersetzt würden (Beispiel: statt
  Gruppe, Gemeinschaft, Mannschaft nur noch *Team*).

- Bei anderen Varianten, die stark ins Irrationale spielen,
  wird die Sprache als Bauwerk, Kunstwerk, organisches
  Wesen oder Person betrachtet, und je nach Metapher ist
  von 'beschädigen, zerstören, beschmutzen, verletzen,
  mißhandeln oder beleidigen' die Rede.

- Mit dem Gebrauch von Anglizismen, vor allem den selbst-
  gemachten, mache man sich vor Briten und Amerikanern
  lächerlich.

- Eine Variante hierzu ist die Besorgnis, die sprachliche
  Anbiederung an die Amerikaner sei würdelos.

- Mehrfach variiert wird das Thema, daß durch Gebrauch von
  Anglizismen soziale Gruppen voneinander abgegrenzt
  würden.

- Darunter ist die Befürchtung durchaus ernst zu nehmen, daß
  durch übertriebene Entlehnung aus dem Englischen und die
  fachsprachliche Abwandlung der Wortbedeutungen die Verständigung zwischen Fachleuten verschiedener Gebiete sowie
  zwischen Fachleuten und Laien immer schwerer würde. Dies
  ist jedoch ein weiterreichendes Fachsprachenproblem, das
  nicht nur mit Anglizismen zusammenhängt.

- Ebenfalls nicht abwegig ist die Sorge, daß durch Anglizismen, die vor allem von der mittleren und jüngeren

Generation gebraucht würden, die Verständigung mit
älteren Menschen beeinträchtigt werde.

- Durch Anglizismen in der Werbe- und Verkaufssprache werde
  nicht informiert, sondern verschleiert.

- Deutschlernenden Ausländern werde durch die vielen Anglizismen der Lernerfolg erschwert. Da sich diese Kritik-
  begründung in mehreren Briefen anglophoner Ausländer findet,
  sind vermutlich vor allem die Pseudoentlehnungen und
  Mischbildungen gemeint.

- Kurios ist die Begründung: Die Entlehnung von derart
  vielen Wörtern aus dem Englischen sei nicht fair, nicht
  ausgewogen, da Briten und Amerikaner im Gegenzug nur sehr
  wenig Wörter aus dem Deutschen entlehnten.

- Das Eindringen von immer mehr Anglizismen gefährde die
  nationale Identität.

- Durchaus ernst gemeint war die Befürchtung, mit dem zu-
  nehmenden Gebrauch von Amerikanismen, also den Entlehnungen aus dem amerikanischen Englisch werde die deutsche
  Wiedervereinigung gefährdet.

Diese Begründung hat Ähnlichkeit mit der Sorge, die nationale
Identität könne verloren gehen. In diesem Fall bin ich übrigens
über meine kleine Textsammlung hinausgegangen. Die Befürchtung
einer Gefährdung der deutschen Wiedervereinigung durch Anglizismen
habe ich nicht in Briefen oder Sprachglossen gefunden, sondern
in einem Zeitungsbericht über einen 1980 gegründeten Verein, die
'Gesellschaft für Kultur, Sitten und Sprache' in Düsseldorf.
Auf die sprachpolitische Einstellung dieser Gesellschaft will ich
hier nicht weiter eingehen. Aus sprachkritischen Arbeiten der
DDR wie auch aus den Beobachtungen des schwedischen Germanisten
Göran Kristensson (1979) läßt sich ersehen, daß auch die DDR
reichlich mit Anglizismen gesegnet ist. Bestätigt wird dies
auch durch die Arbeiten meines Mannheimer Kollegen Manfred
Hellmann zur Entwicklung des Wortschatzes in den beiden deutschen
Sprachen.

Zu (3): Vorgeschlagene Maßnahmen

Die Düsseldorfer 'Gesellschaft für Kultur, Sitten und Sprache' erwähne ich nur deshalb, weil sie mir einen Übergang zur Frage (3) nach den von den Sprachkritikern geforderten Konsequenzen ermöglicht. Von dieser Gesellschaft kommt nämlich die entschiedenste Forderung, nämlich nach einer gesetzlichen Regelung. Seit rund zwei Jahren appelliert der Vorsitzende dieses mitgliederschwachen Vereins, Friedrich Fuhrmann, an den Bundestag, an Minister, den Kanzler und den Bundespräsidenten, ein Gesetz zur Reinigung des Deutschen von überflüssigen Fremdwörtern einzubringen. Von den neuen Aktionen erfahren wir in Mannheim jeweils über Anfragen von Presse und Radio. Wir werden dann meist gefragt, was wir von Herrn Fuhrmanns Gesetzesvorschlag halten. Natürlich nichts.

Anders als bei den vielfältigen Begründungen für ihre negative Einstellung zu Anglizismen und Entlehnungen aus anderen Sprachen haben die sprachkritischen Briefschreiber und Journalisten nur wenige konkrete Vorschläge zur Änderung der kritisierten Verhältnisse zu machen.

Die Forderung nach einem Sprachreinigungsgesetz wurde schon erwähnt. Zu ergänzen ist hierzu, daß in vielen Zeitungsartikeln außerhalb meines kleinen Korpus, die sich mit den Sprachreinigungsbestrebungen in Frankreich befassen, sich nicht nur Schadenfreude und verhaltenem Spott über das Gesetz Bas-Lauriol vom 31.12.1975 findet, das den Gebrauch französischer Wörter in mehreren Bereichen der Öffentlichkeit zwingend vorschreibt. Gelegentlich, wenn auch selten, trifft man auch verhaltene Bewunderung oder gar Neid auf die Franzosen, die auf diese Weise von den Anglizismen befreit werden bzw. befreit werden sollten.

In anderen Leserbriefen und Schreiben an unser Institut wird wiederholt gefordert, daß vor allem die sprachlichen Multiplikatoren, also die Rundfunk- und Fernsehanstalten, die Politiker, die Verleger und Schriftsteller auf ihren Sprachgebrauch achten und Fremdwörter möglichst vermeiden. Appelliert wird auch an

Universitäten und Schulen. Von unserem Institut wurden wiederholt Richtlinien für einen guten fremdwortarmen Sprachgebrauch
verlangt.

Zweifellos sinnvoll aber nicht bloß wegen der Anglizismen
ist der Vorschlag, in Tageszeitungen, Funk und Fernsehen ständige
Sparten 'Sprachkritik', eventuell gekoppelt mit der Sparte 'Werbe-
kritik', einzurichten. In anderen Briefen ist eher eine unklare
Suche nach einer Autorität, einer verläßlichen normativen Instanz
zu erkennen, die das Anglizismenproblem für den verwirrten oder
verärgerten Einzelnen löst. Hier nur ein kurzes Zitat:

> Wer hat zum Beispiel entschieden, daß *Show* und *Lobby*
> weiblich sind? Entscheidet darüber das Parlament in
> Bonn, oder haben Sie ein Äquivalent zur Academie
> Française? Wer entscheidet, wann amerikanische Haupt-
> wörter *der*, *die* oder *das* sollen? Wer hat entschieden,
> daß *Computer der* ist ebenso wie *der Thriller* oder *der
> Tramp* oder *der Trenchcoat*? Und sind sicher in diesen
> Tagen der weiblichen Befreiung, daß Sie wirklich *der
> Boss* sagen sollten?

Interessanterweise stammen mehrere Briefe von Deutschameri-
kanern oder Deutschen, die sich längere Zeit im Ausland aufge-
halten haben. Von ihnen gehen ganz generelle Appelle aus wie
z.B.:

> *Tut etwas liebe Landsleute!*

Keine Maßnahmen werden in der Regel von den Autoren der Sprachglossen in den Zeitungen angeboten oder vorgeschlagen, und das
leuchtet auch unmittelbar ein, weil diese Journalisten ihr eigenes
sprachkritisches Tun als konkrete Maßnahme ansehen.

Noch ein kurzer Blick auf die abgewogenen oder gar positiven
Sprachglossen zur Fremdwortfrage. Für die Ermittlung von Einstellungen zu Anglizismen geben diese Texte längst nicht soviel
her wie die negativen Stellungnahmen, und zwar schon deshalb
nicht, weil positiv wertende oder abwägende Texte meist emotions-
ärmer und damit auch sprachlich weniger interessant sind.

Bei den wenigen Texten dieser Art in meiner Sammlung ist zu
unterscheiden zwischen Hinweisen auf den 'richtigen' Gebrauch,
die 'richtige' Aussprache oder Schreibweise von Entlehnungen und

generellen Betrachtungen über den Nutzen von Wörtern, die aus anderen Sprachen übernommen sind.

Zu den Belehrungen gehört eine Glosse, in der darauf hinge-wiesen wird, daß zweisilbige Entlehnungen aus dem Englischen wie *Knowhow*, *Blackout*, *Makeup* und *Comeback* oft falsch betont werden: *Knowhów*, *Blackoút*, *Makeúp* und *Comebáck*. Und dies solle man, bittesehr nicht tun. Ich halte dies, nebenbei gesagt, nicht für einen besonders guten Rat.

Ein Beispiel für die Betrachtungen über die relative Nütz-lichkeit von entlehnten Wörtern ist eine der wöchentlichen Glossen von Rudolf Walter Leonhard in der ZEIT (vom 4.11.1982). Er gibt zu, daß Einzelfälle von Fremdwortmißbrauch vorkommen, hält aber Fremdwörter unter drei Bedingungen für notwendig oder zulässig:

- 'wo es ein entsprechendes deutsches Wort nicht gibt.'
  (Beispiel: *Colleges* in England)

- 'wo Lokalkolorit vermittelt werden soll.'
  (Beispiel: *Datscha* in der Sowjetunion)

- 'wo es die Stilebene einer Aussage bestimmt'
  (Beispiel: *Chic einer raffinierten femme fatale*)

Ob diese Empfehlung besonders sinnvoll und praktisch ist (Ich hätte Probleme vor allem mit der dritten Bedingung), möchte ich nicht diskutieren. Dieses Beispiel sollte lediglich ver-deutlichen, daß sich aus Sprachglossen auch auf positive Ein-stellungen zu Entlehnungen aus anderen Sprachen schließen läßt.

Der kurze Überblick und der Versuch einer ersten Ordnung und Sichtung von Sprachanfragen, Leserbriefen und Sprachglossen gestattet noch keine verläßlichen Verallgemeinerungen. Die wenigen Texte erlauben allenfalls Vermutungen über die verschied-enen Arten von Einstellungen zu Anglizismen. Ich hoffe aber, daß es mir möglich war zu zeigen, daß sich eine gründliche Aus-wertung eines erheblich größeren Corpus derartiger Texte lohnt. Mühsam ist zunächst vor allem die Beschaffung von mehr Texten. Es gibt aber mehrere Stellen, bei denen man mit Hilfe rechnen kann.

Das IdS, also unser Institut kann nicht sehr viel bieten, da es
sich seit einiger Zeit herumgesprochen hat, daß wir keine routine-
mäßige Sprachberatung bieten. Reichhaltiger sind mit Sicherheit
das Archiv der Sprachberatungsstelle der Duden-Redaktion, und
fündig wird man wohl auch bei der Gesellschaft für deutsche Sprache
in Wiesbaden werden. Was die Leserbriefe und Sprachglossen in
den Zeitungen angeht, so wird man recht viel eigene Sucharbeit
investieren müssen, da nur wenige Zeitschriften über ein gut
organisiertes Archiv wie der 'Spiegel' verfügen. Auf verhält-
nismäßig einfache Art ließe sich das Corpus erweitern durch die
Anfragen, Antworten und Glossen, die in den verschiedenen Zeitschriften für Sprachpflege erscheinen, vor allem den Zeitschriften
Muttersprache, Sprachdienst und *Der Sprachpfleger* in der Bundesrepublik und der *Sprachpflege,* die in der DDR erscheint.

Warum ich Ihnen dies alles erzähle, sollte nicht schwer zu
erraten sein. Mit den Anglizismen tun wir deutschen Germanisten
uns meist etwas schwer, und zwar auch wenn wir etwas Englisch
können. Mit dem Schwertun meine ich weniger emotionale Einstellungen, mit denen einige von uns Probleme haben; ich meine
damit vor allem die verminderte Fähigkeit, bestimmte Arten von
Lehnprägungen im Deutschen zu erkennen und den Abstand zu be-
urteilen, den Entlehnungen nach ihrer Übernahme ins Deutsche zur
Gebersprache aufweisen. Die Erforschung von Anglizismen sollte
deshalb eine naheliegende Aufgabe für englische Germanisten sein,
vielleicht auch in Zusammenarbeit mit dem einen oder anderen
deutschen Kollegen.

Lassen Sie mich zum Abschluß auf den zweiten Forschungs-
bereich eingehen, in dem nach meinem Eindruck noch viel Arbeit
zu leisten ist, und den ich mit der stark vereinfachenden Frage
benennen will: Wie lange leben welche Anglizismen?

Sofern ich die einschlägige Literatur richtig gelesen habe,
gilt besonders seit der zweiten Hälfte des letzten Jahrhunderts,
daß jährlich, neuerdings vielleicht sogar alle paar Monate, einige
Ausdrücke aus dem britischen oder amerikanischen Englisch (im
Einzelfall ist das offensichtlich schwer zu entscheiden) auf kaum

vorhersagbare Weise in den deutschsprachigen Ländern in Gebrauch
kommen und dann auf ebensowenig vorhersehbare Weise rasch oder
langsam wieder verschwinden oder aber bleiben und dann mehr oder
weniger stark phonologisch und morphologisch integriert werden.

Um nur wenige Beispiele aus der jüngeren Vergangenheit zu
erwähnen: Was ein *Teach-in* ist, wissen die heutigen Studenten
kaum noch. *Beatnik*, *hip* und *Hipster* sind längst überholt. *Band*
als Bezeichnung für mehrere zusammenspielende Unterhaltungsmusiker
ist ebenfalls kaum mehr im Gebrauch, es sei denn in der Zusammen-
setzung *Bigband*. Heute ist stattdessen nur noch von *Gruppe* die
Rede. Mit dem Tanz ist auch das Wort *Twist* trotz einiger Wieder-
belebungsversuche aus der Mode gekommen. Seitdem neuerdings
fast jeder Käseladen *Boutique* heißt, ist auch das noch vor wenigen
Jahren so beliebte *shop* auf dem Rückzug. *Shopping* geht man
ohnehin nur noch in der Vorstellung einiger weniger Modezeit-
schriften. Die Sache selbst heißt längst wieder *Einkaufen* oder
Einkaufsbummel.

Andererseits haben uns die letzten Jahre auch außerhalb der
Fach- und Sondersprachen eine Reihe häufig gebrauchter Anglizismen
gebracht, darunter *Allrounder*, *Job-Sharing*, *Holocaust*, *Recycling*,
Midlife-Krise (eine interessante Mischform) und *Walkman*, vor
kurzem auch *Aerobic*; von *Jogging* wird entsprechend weniger
gesprochen.

In einem Teil solcher Fälle ist es ohne weiteres plausibel,
daß der Gebrauch der Wörter mit den Sachen, die sie bezeichnen,
beginnt und endet. Es gibt aber durchaus Gegenbeispiele, wo die
Sachen bleiben, aber die Wörter sich ändern oder geändert werden,
also etwa *Laden : Shop : Boutique*. Besonders originell wirkt
es, wenn einzelne Geschäfte sich (wieder) als *Laden* bezeichnen
(z.B. *Hosenladen*, *Kleiderladen* u.a.).

Was in der Anglizismenforschung, soweit ich sie übersehe,
bisher noch fehlt, das sind größere Untersuchungen zur Abnutzungsrate von Entlehnungen aus dem Englischen. Ich will hierzu nur
noch einige Beispiele für Entlehnungen geben, die weiter zurück-
liegen.

Ich beziehe mich hierbei auf Angaben in sprachkritischen
Schriften der Jahrhundertwende, besonders auf Dunger (1909).
Damals dauerte die eifrige Entlehnung aus dem Englischen, die
im letzten Viertel des 19. Jahrhunderts immer stärker geworden
war, noch an. Ich habe Ausdrücke in verschiedenen Lebens-
bereichen gesucht, die in der Gegenwartssprache nicht mehr gebräuch-
lich sind, und bin sehr schnell fündig geworden. Hier nur eine
kleine Auswahl von inzwischen ungebräuchlich gewordenen Entlehnungen:

Dinner *(Mittag- oder Abendessen)*

Sandwich *(belegtes Brot, Schnittchen)*

Jam (Marmelade oder *Konfitüre)*

Garden-Party *(Gartenfest* oder auch *Gartenparty)*

Racket *(Schläger)*

Dining-Car *(Speisewagen)*

Vacuum-Cleaner *(Staubsauger)*

Mackintosh *(Regenmantel)*

Cast-Steel *(Gußstahl)*

Nurse *(Kindermädchen)*

Groom *(Reitknecht)* falls überhaupt

Bill *(Gesetzesvorlage/Vorlage)*

Adresse *(Grußbotschaft/Ansprache)*

Minorität *(Minderheit)*

Affidavit *(eidesstattliche Erklärung)* nur noch in spez.
Gebrauch

Wie diese wenigen Beispiele zeigen, sind die nicht mehr ge-
brauchten Entlehnungen auf unterschiedliche Weise ersetzt worden:
etwa durch Lehnbildungen wie bei *cast-steel* durch *Gußstahl, Dining-
Car* durch *Speisewagen,* durch ältere Entlehnungen aus anderen
Sprachen wie bei *Jam* durch *Marmelade/Konfitüre* oder durch komplexe
Ausdrücke, die in keine erkennbaren Beziehung zum Englischen
stehen, wie etwa bei *Vacuum Cleaner* durch *Staubsauger* oder bei *Bill*
durch *Gesetzesvorlage.*

Aufschlußreich wären diachronische Untersuchungen anhand
umfangreicher Datenerhebungen, bei denen die Gebrauchsdauer, die

Art des Austausches bzw. der Abänderung von Entlehnungen und die
Lebensbereiche, in denen die betreffenden Ausdrücke gebraucht
werden, korreliert würden. Entsprechende Verfahren ließen sich
mit Modifikationen aus Glottochronologie und anderen Arten der
Lexikostatistik übernehmen. Damit gerate ich aber in den Bereich
spekulativer Forschungsplanung. Wenn ich den Gedanken trotzdem
noch ein bißchen weiterspinnen darf:

Im Unterschied zu den Entlehnungen aus anderen Sprachen, vor
allem Latein, Griechisch und Französisch, kam es zu den großen
Entlehnungswellen aus dem Englischen erst in neuerer Zeit, also
seit dem letzten Jahrhundert. Es ist also reichlich Quellen-
material vorhanden, in gut gestreuten unterschiedlichen Textsorten:
Trivialliteratur, Zeitungstexte, Fachtexte, Übersetzungen, aus
der Nachkriegszeit sogar reichhaltige Aufzeichnungen gesprochener
Texte, und zwar sowohl in der Gebersprache Englisch wie in der
Nehmersprache Deutsch. Damit besteht eine Gelegenheit, wie sie
sonst in der Sprachgeschichte nie gegeben war, dem Phänomen der
Entlehnung unter quantitativen und qualitativen Gesichtspunkten
empirisch auf den Grund zu gehen. Anders als bei herkömmlichen
Wortschatzuntersuchungen würden nicht lediglich mehr oder weniger
isolierte Geschichten einzelner Wörter leidlich geordnet zusammen-
gefaßt, sondern auf quantitativem Weg auch die Bedingungen, die
funktionale Bedeutung und die relative Stabilität der verschiedenen
Entlehnungsarten ermittelt. Die große Belegsammlung von Broder
Carstensen müßte sich neben ihrer lexikographischen Auswertung
auch für diesen Zweck verwenden lassen. Mittel und Verfahren
für die Bewältigung weiterer Datenmengen sind inzwischen verfüg-
bar. Da die Lesecomputer neuerdings auch für sehr verschiedene
Schriftarten programmierbar sind, stellt selbst die Aufnahme der
Belegtexte für die Rohbearbeitung mit dem Computer kein so großes
Problem mehr dar wie noch vor wenigen Jahren. In der Diskussion
gleich lasse ich mir gern linguistischen Größenwahn oder Abenteuer-
lust vorwerfen.

Daß derartige großflächige Wortschatzuntersuchungen sinnvoll
und möglich sind, versucht eine kleine Arbeitsgruppe im Institut

für deutsche Sprache schon seit mehreren Jahren zu zeigen, wobei aber Anglizismen nur eine marginale Rolle spielen. Seit rund 19 Jahren beobachten einige meiner Kollegen die Entwicklung des Wortschatzes des öffentlichen Sprachgebrauchs in der Bundesrepublik und in der DDR. Dabei geht es um die Erfassung der Gemeinsamkeiten und Unterschiede der Wortschatzentwicklungen in dem eingegrenzten Beobachtungsbereich. Ich will auf dieses Projekt hier nicht weiter eingehen, weil es dabei vor allem um die Überprüfung der Frage geht, ob sich ein und dieselbe Sprache unter verschiedenen soziopolitischen und ökonomischen Bedingungen unterschiedlich entwickelt. Interessant ist das Projekt in unserem thematischen Zusammenhang nur, weil es Verfahren zur quantitativen Bearbeitung großer Wortmengen auch unter kurzdiachronischen Aspekten entwickelt hat.

Die skizzierte Forschungsaufgabe 'Wie lange leben welche Anglizismen?' wäre sozusagen die diachronische Entsprechung zur synchronischen Einstellungsforschung. Es war ja stets vor allem die Angst vor der vermuteten großen Menge der Entlehnungen, die als Begründung für die negative Einstellung zu den entlehnten Einheiten angegeben wurde. Ich zitiere aus einer Erklärung, die 1899 von der Hauptversammlung des Allgemeinen Deutschen Sprachvereins auf Vorschlag von Herrmann Dunger (s. Dunger 1909, Vorwort) einstimmig angenommen wurde:

> Mit dem immer wachsenden Einfluß englischen Wesens mehrt sich neuerdings in bedenklicher Weise die Zahl der aus dem Englischen stammenden Fremdwörter. Auch in dieser Spracherscheinung treten die alten Erbfehler des deutschen Volkes wieder hervor: Überschätzung des Fremden, Mangel an Selbstgefühl, Mißachtung der eigenen Sprache.

Wenn das Wort *englisch* in diesem Textstück durch *amerikanisch* ersetzt würde, könnte es auch aus einem der Leserbriefe aus neuester Zeit stammen. Die Angst vor der großen Zahl der Entlehnungen ist geradezu ein Topos in der Begründung negativer Einstellungen. Als Linguisten müssen wir zugeben, daß wir über die Anzahl der Entlehnungen, über die Bedingungen und Umfang ihrer Abnutzung bzw. ihrer dauerhaften Integration nur wenig wissen.

Ein solches Wissen ließe sich über die skizzierten umfangreichen
diachronischen Forschungen gewinnen. Sie würden unter anderem
dazu beitragen, unbegründete oder nur irrational motivierte Fehl-
einschätzungen und Vorurteile abzubauen.

Literaturverzeichnis

Betz, W. (1945) 'Die Lehnbildungen und der abendländische
   Sprachausgleich'. In: *Beiträge zur Geschichte der deutschen
   Sprache und Literatur* 67, 275-302.

Braun, P. (Hrsg.) (1979) *Fremdwortdiskussion*. (= UTB 797),
   München.

Carstensen, B. (1965) *Englische Einflüsse auf die deutsche Sprache
   nach 1945*. Heidelberg.

Carstensen, B. (1979) 'Evidente und latente Einflüsse des
   Englischen auf das Deutsche'. In: P. Braun (Hrsg.), 90-94.

Carstensen, B. (1979) Zur Intensität und Rezeption des englischen
   Einflusses. In: P. Braun (Hrsg.) 321-326.

Carstensen, B., Galinsky, H. (1975) *Amerikanismen der deutschen
   Gegenwartssprache: Entlehnungsvorgänge und stilistische
   Aspekte*. 3. verb. Auflage, Heidelberg.

Clyne, M.G. (1973) 'Kommunikation und Kommunikationsbarrieren bei
   englischen Entlehnungen im heutigen Deutsch'. In:
   Zeitschrift für Germanistische Linguistik 1, 163-177.

Duckworth, D. (1970) 'Der Einfluß des Englischen auf den deutschen
   Wortschatz seit 1945'. In: *Zeitschrift für deutsche Sprache*
   26, 9-31 (auch in: Braun, 212-245).

Dunger, H. (1909) *Engländerei in der deutschen Sprache*. Berlin.

Fink, H. (1970) *Amerikanismen im Wortschatz der deutschen Tages-
   presse, dargestellt am Beispiel dreier überregionaler
   Zeitungen*. Diss. Mainz 1968. Teilabdruck als: *Mainzer
   Amerikanische Beiträge* 11.

Fink, H. (1980) '*Superhit* oder *Spitzenschlager*: Ein Versuch zur
   Häufigkeit und Funktion von Anglizismen und "Werbeanglizismen"
   in deutschen Jugendzeitschriften'. In: H. Viereck (Hrsg.),
   185-212.

Galinsky, H. (1972) *Amerikanisch-deutsche Sprach- und Literatur-
   beziehungen. Systematische Übersicht und Forschungsbericht
   1945-1970*. Frankfurt.

Hellmann, M.W. (Hrsg.) *Ost-West-Wortschatzvergleiche* (=
   Forschungsberichte des Instituts fur deutsche Sprache Bd. 48).
   Tübingen (im Druck).

Kristensson, G. (1979) 'Angloamerikanische Einflüsse in DDR-Zeitungstexten'. In: Braun, 327-336.

Kuhn, H. (1971) 'Ergänzende Beobachtungen zu Lehnsyntax, Lehnwendung und Lehnbedeutung'. In: *Fragen der strukturellen Syntax und der kontrastiven Grammatik* (= *Sprache der Gegenwart* Bd. 17), hrsg. v. H. Moser et al., Düsseldorf.

Langner, H. (1980/81) 'Zum Einfluß des Angloamerikanischen auf die deutsche Sprache der Gegenwart'. In: *Sprachpflege* 29, 69-73.

Polenz, P.V. (1967) 'Fremdwort und Lehnwort sprachwissenschaftlich betrachtet'. In: *Muttersprache*, 1967, H. 3/4. (auch in P. Braun, 9-31).

Stanforth, A.W. (1968) 'Deutsch-englischer Lehnwortaustausch'. In: *Wortgeographie und Gesellschaft. Festgabe für L.E. Schmitt*, hrsg. von W. Mitzka. Berlin, 526-560.

Viereck, W. (Hrsg.) (1980) *Studien zum Einfluß der englischen Sprache auf das Deutsche.* Tübingen.

Viereck, W. (1980) 'Empirische Untersuchungen insbesondere zum Verständnis und Gebrauch von Anglizismen im Deutschen'. In: W. Viereck (Hrsg.), 238-321.

Viereck, K., Viereck, W., Winter, I. (1975) 'Wie englisch ist unsere Pressesprache?' *Grazer Linguistische Studien* 2, 205-226.

SLAVONIC INFLUENCES ON HIGH GERMAN IN AUSTRIA AND THE GERMAN
DEMOCRATIC REPUBLIC

Graham D.C. Martin
(Department of Modern Languages, University of Strathclyde, Glasgow)

Abbreviations referring to languages

Cz.	= Czech		Sb.Cr.	= Serbo-Croat
Pol.	= Polish		Sorb.	= Sorbian
Russ.	= Russian		Ukr.	= Ukrainian

I   General

The German-speaking area is, and always has been, flanked to
the east by largely Slavonic territory.   If we have a look at
the present-day politico-linguistic map we find that three German-
speaking states are contiguous with four different Slavonic
languages: Polish takes up most of the border with the German
Democratic Republic (GDR), from the Baltic coast southwards; Czech
forms an indentation in German-speaking territory, linking the
south-east of the GDR, a north-easterly strip of Bavaria (Federal
Republic of Germany) and the north-east of Austria; its close
relation, Slovak, continues for a short further strip of north-
east Austria, before Hungarian cuts into Slavonic territory and
occupies the eastern border with Austria; finally Slovene meets
the south-east border of Austria for a considerable length.

Within present-day German-speaking territory there are, moreover, a number of Slavonic enclaves, most notably Sorbian (with
its Upper and Lower varieties) in Lusatia (GDR).   On a smaller
scale are the Slovene enclaves in Carinthia (Austria) and a few
minor Croat settlements in Burgenland (Austria).

Political and demographic shifts in the course of time brought German into further forms of contact with certain of the above-mentioned languages. In the early Middle Ages Sorbian occupied a much larger area than today, and was a neighbour rather than an enclave in relation to German; some centuries later Polish was also a language of certain constituent parts of the Austrian Empire. Two further Slavonic languages, Serbo-Croat and Ukrainian, were spoken by peoples belonging to the far-flung Austrian Empire, while on the Baltic coast Pomoranian[1] surrounded the then German city of Danzig.

Peters (1968 : 624) maintains that exchanges between the neighbouring Germanic and Slavonic peoples were, compared with similar cases of adjacent cultures, exceptionally intensive in the course of many centuries. Particularly striking is the number of population shifts between Germanic and Slavonic tribes in the early Middle Ages in the territory we know today as eastern Germany and western Poland, whereby Slavonic tribes pushed Germanic tribes westwards at one stage, only to be pushed back eastwards again at a later stage by the Germans - a shuttling process which was repeated in the course of time. The gradual German *Ostkolonisation* during the Middle Ages fixed the boundaries between the two language groups for many centuries to come, until the Poles and Czechs regained some of their ancient territories as recently as 1945.

As a result of so much political activity and cultural contact, a fair amount of linguistic interaction would seem inevitable. In fact, however, as many authorities acknowledge, the linguistic intercourse has been a largely one-sided affair, in that countless German influences have been absorbed by Slavonic languages (even in Russian, as long-distance loans), but relatively few Slavonic ones have made an impact on German.

As far as the standard German language is concerned, even lexical items of Slavonic origin in everyday use and referring to indigenous conditions are distinctly limited in number. As cited in all the standard histories of the language, a batch of

nouns which form fundamental items of modern German vocabulary
came in between about the thirteenth and sixteenth centuries.
Many historians of German are either vague or contradict one
another as to which Slavonic language gave rise to which word in
German, but Bielfeldt (1965) has performed an admirable task in
providing clarity and precision in this respect.[2] These nouns
include: *Grenze* (earliest occurrence in the thirteenth century;
Pol. *granica*); *Quark* (fourteenth century; Pol. *twaróg*, Lower
Sorb.[3] *twarog*); *Peitsche* (fourteenth century; Cz. *bič*, Sorb. *bič*,
Pol. *bicz*[4]). *Gurke* (sixteenth century) probably comes from Pol.
ogórek (perhaps reinforced by Cz. *okurka*). *Jauche* is another
old loan, whose complex origins are unduly simplified by most
authorities, who refer only to an Old Slavonic or Old Polish word
jucha meaning 'soup'; Bielfeldt (1965 : 40ff.) points to a double
origin in German, whereby the usage from the fifteenth century on
with that meaning is confined to certain dialects, while the later
standard use in the sense of 'liquid manure' has its nearest Slavonic equivalent in Sorb. *jucha*.[5]

From about the twelfth to the fourteenth century a number of
words referring to items such as furs, song-birds and berries found
their way into German from various Slavonic languages. During
the fifteenth and sixteenth century Czech gave rise to a batch of
terms with mainly military associations. From that time on,
Slavonic loans which have established themselves in truly everyday use in standard German are few and far between. Russ. *droški*
(a plural form) produced the German *Droschke*, which became an
everyday word in German usage from late eighteenth century on.
Many authorities claim a Russian origin (*chrip*) for *Grippe* (from
the late eighteenth century, though Kluge (1967 : 271) specifically refutes this and suggests the French root *grippe* instead.
The colloquial exclamation *dalli*, 'on the double' coming from Pol.
dalej, spread to various parts from Berlin in particular from the
late nineteenth century. In our own time, the colloquial term
Apparatschik (Russ. *apparatčik*) and the popular jargon prefix
Polit- (Russ. *polit-*, a clipping from the adjective *političeskij*)
have entered German direct from Russian. Otherwise the vast

majority of Slavonic words known in German are exoticisms referring to conditions in the country of origin, or else they belong
to technical spheres.

II   Austria

From the Middle Ages on, Austrian (i.e. Habsburg) domains came
to embrace an increasing number of Slavonic territories.   Not long
before the collapse of the Austro-Hungarian state at the end of the
First World War, a census taken in 1910 showed that the territories
of the Dual Monarchy contained as many as 23.5m Slavs (45% of the
population), along with 12m German speakers (23%) and 10m Magyars
(19%) (Taylor 1964 : 286).   The largest Slavonic nation within
Habsburg domains, and the one with which Austria had by far the
strongest cultural links, was the Czechs, who occupied Bohemia,
Moravia and part of Silesia.   The political and cultural axis Vienna-
Prague was important for many centuries up to the end of the First
World War.   In those times there were many Czech immigrant workers
employed in Austria, and there was a sizeable Czech colony estab-
lished in Vienna (as well as a large German-speaking colony in
Prague).   The second greatest cultural link was probably with the
Slovenes (occupying Carniola and Gorizia), although in numbers they
ranked fourth amongst the Slavonic peoples in Austrian provinces.

The other Slavonic races, though in some cases forming a
numerous population, occupied more distant parts of the vast Austrian territories.   Poles constituted the second largest Slavonic
nation within the Austrian Empire, and Polish was spoken in much
of Galicia and part of Silesia.   Next came Ukrainian (also known
historically as Ruthenian), spoken in the rest of Galicia and part
of Bukovina.   Finally, Serbo-Croat was the language of the provinces of Dalmatia and Istria.

Austria obtained second-degree links with further Slavonic
parts through the union with the Hungarian crown from 1867 on.
Slovakia (whose capital, Bratislava, is situated very near to the

Austrian border) was a Hungarian domain.   Links with Serbo-Croat
culture were strengthened through contacts with Croatia-Slavonia,
and those with Ukrainian through the population speaking that tongue
in the Hungarian Carpathians.

Internal connections between the modern Austrian state and
Slavonic peoples come through the Slovene minority in the population of Carinthia and the Croat pockets in Burgenland, as well
as through the fact that there are large numbers of Yugoslavian
immigrant workers (mostly Serbo-Croat speakers) employed throughout Austria.

With such widespread and long-standing geographical and
historical, political and cultural links, one would expect to
find a variety of Slavonic influences on the German language used
in Austria.   In fact such influences almost exclusively affect
the lexical sphere, at least as far as the standard language is
concerned.   Even here the largest number of items are to be found
in the realm of gastronomy[6], which I intend to exclude from consideration because of its specialised nature.

Many culinary terms come from Czech, but in view of the exceptionally strong former cultural links, there are otherwise very
few instances of definite loans from Czech in basic standard
Austrian vocabulary.   As a partial exception one might cite the
word *Hetschepetsch* (f.) meaning 'rose-hip'.   This comes from
standard Cz. *šípek*, and particularly from a dialect.variant *hečipeč*
(cf. Rizzo-Baur 1962 : 85).   The reduplication of sounds would
seem to give the word an almost frivolous ring and a dialectal
flavour;   an Austrian (Styrian) informant tells me that he would
associate the word with children's speech, yet the *Österreichisches
Wörterbuch* (1979) notes standard German *Hagebutte* as being unusual
in Austria.[7]

Slovene provides a word that is undoubtedly one of the most
typical lexical peculiarities of the Austrian regional standard:
Jause (f.).   The Slovene origin is *južina*, for which many dictionaries give the meaning of 'lunch', though a Slovene-speaking
informant tells me he knows it best in the sense of a 'between-

meal snack'.   In Austrian usage it may refer to either a mid-
morning or a mid-afternoon snack, though there are probably stronger
associations with the afternoon.   It was an early loan in German,
the earliest example being known from the fifteenth century with
a MHG monophthong: *jūs* (Kluge 1967 : 331; Ebner 1969 : 254).
In spite of competition from a word of Italian origin (*Marende*)
in the dialects of the western provinces, *Jause* is in common use
in virtually all of present-day Austria; even in the Alemannic-
speaking Vorarlberg, this lexical import from the far south-east
of the country is frequently seen in print in local use.   Conversely, with the exception of a small part of south-east Bavaria
adjoining Austria, the word seems to be largely confined to Austria
in normal High German usage (cf. Kretschmer 1969 : 551f.).

The word *Jause* is such a basic item of Austrian vocabulary
that it gives rise to numerous compounds, in both directions,
e.g. *Jausenbrot, -kaffee, -station, -zeit; Salami-, Vieruhrjause.*
Further proof of the basic nature of the word *Jause* is afforded by
its very frequent occurrence, in various permutations, in the works
of many well-known Austrian authors, such as H.C. Artmann, Heimito
von Doderer, Peter Handke, Ernst Jandl, Karl Kraus, and Arthur
Schnitzler.

Connected with the noun *Jause* is the verb *jausnen* (Slovene
južinati), with its less common variant *jausen.*

A word of Turkish origin which came into Austrian German usage
via Slavonic parts only in the nineteenth century is *Kukuruz* (m.),
meaning 'maize'.   Sb.Cr. *kukuruz* is the nearest Slavonic form,
but even if that was the origin of German *Kukuruz,* it would seem
possible that cognate forms such as Cz. *kukuřice,* Slovak *kukurica*
and Pol. *kukuryca* reinforced Austrian adoption of the term.   This
word, too, can be found in the works of Austrian authors, such as
H.C. Artmann, Thomas Bernhard, Karl Kraus, and Joseph Roth.   In
spite of its somewhat ungainly sound, this noun lends itself to
compounds such as *Kukuruzfeld* and *-kolben.*

Some doubt surrounds the exact origin of another very common
Austrian word: *Kren* (m.), meaning 'horseradish'.   There is no

doubt that the origin is Slavonic, and many authorities seem to indicate a common Slavonic origin. Every Slavonic language with connections with Austria does indeed contain this lexical item: Cz. *křen*, Slovak *chren*, Slovene *hren*, Sb.Cr. *hren*, Ukr. *chrín*, Pol. *chrzan*. Since the word is also to be found in east-central and even some north-eastern dialects of German, Bielfeldt (1965 : 45) treats this word under Sorbian influences (cf. modern Sorb. *chrěn*). Seibicke (1972 : 77f.) refers to a former occurrence in almost the whole of the east of the German-speaking area, but maintains that nowadays the word is largely an Austrian peculiarity. However, informants from Bavaria have stated that it is common use in various parts of eastern Bavaria and also in Munich. The occurrence throughout Austria and also in eastern Bavaria would surely seem to indicate a strong Czech influence in those parts, reinforced perhaps in the south east of Austria by the Slovene form. German written usage goes back to MHG times, when the alternative forms *krēn* and *chrēn* occur (the latter being phonetically closer to Old Cz. *chrěn*, as well as the form in all the other Slavonic languages with an initial fricative rather than a plosive).

Culturally, *Kren* is a relatively more important concept in Austria than its standard German semantic equivalent *Meerettich* (which is practically never used in Austria) elsewhere, in that it is consumed much more frequently in those parts (e.g. as a relish instead of mustard with *Würstl*). This fact, together with the linguistic factor that the word forms a more compact lexical item, leads to its being used figuratively in expressions such as *er hat viel Kren* or *ein Mandl mit Kren* (Kretschmer 1969 : 333f.; Ebner 1969 : 150). It also lends itself to compounding in both directions, e.g. *Krenfleisch* and the doubly Austrian *Oberskren!*

An Austrian lexical item with a morphological peculiarity is the colloquial term *Feschak* (m.; pl. *-s*). Ebner (1969 : 83) gives a double definition for it:

a) fescher, sehr männlich aussehender Kerl;
b) Kamerad, der zu allem aufgelegt ist, überall mittut, nicht fad ist.

This form is an interesting loan hybrid.   The root is the adjective *fesch*, itself a well-known loan from English - a clipping of
fashionable.   Ebner simply gives 'slaw.' as the origin of the
ending, but the most obvious influence would seem to be Czech, where
the suffix *-ák* forms a common ending in nouns referring to people
(e.g. *hlupák* = blockhead; *slovák* = Slovak).   Czech has borrowed
the Anglo-German *fesch* and assimilated it morphologically by adding
a Czech adjectival ending to form *fešný*, which would appear to be
a well-established colloquialism according to Machek's etymological
dictionary of Czech (1957 : 108).   Czech also has an associated
noun form: *fešák*.[8]   Since there seems to be no obvious model in
German with the *-ak* ending on which the Austrians formed their
Feschak[9], it might appear most logical that the Czechs first
borrowed the adjective from German, then formed the noun *fešák*
according their conventional processes of word formation, and that
the Austrians then borrowed the word back again in noun form.
Machek, however, specifically states that Cz. *fešák* came from
'German' *Feschak*!

   The word *Feschak* is reflected in the usage of a number of
Austrian authors.   Karl Kraus shows quite a predilection for it
in his epic play *Die letzten Tage der Menschheit*, though most
instances occur in a dialect context; moreover, one of the myriad
of minor, fleeting characters is 'Ein Feschak'.[10]   Heimito von
Doderer provides a nice specimen in the novel *Die Wasserfälle von
Slunj* in which he gives a definition of the term:[11]

   Er kann als Feschak bezeichnet werden, als ein allzu
   fescher Kerl.

   Even greater etymological and morphological complications
occur with a further derivative of the noun form, the abstract
noun *Feschaktum*, whose elements are clearly of English, Slavonic
(i.e. Czech?) and German origin.

   Austrian usage contains an orthographical peculiarity which
may reflect a Slavonic influence in the case of the spelling of
Zwetschke.   Of the many standard reference works which go into
the etymology of the word *Zwetsch(g)e*, most note the variant spelling usual in Austria without comment; the same is the case with

the works dealing specifically with peculiarities of Austrian
standard usage.   One notable exception is Kluge (1967 : 896),
who cites as an origin the Greek form *damáskēnon,* 'dessen *k* in
Zwetschke bis heute nachwirkt'; however, the words *damáskēnon*
and *Zwetschke* are in all other respects so far apart that the
evidence is hardly convincing.   The *Deutsches Wörterbuch* (XVI,
1104) cites some early written specimens from the sixteenth century
coming from the south-west of the German-speaking area with a *-ke*
ending, but the other variant forms extant and the general ortho-.
graphical instability of that period make it impossible to draw
any definite conclusions in this respect.

I would venture to suggest that the conventional Austrian
spelling with the *-ke* ending may well at least be reinforced by
Slavonic - particularly Czech - influences.   *-ka* is in fact a
common ending for feminine nouns in practically all Slavonic
languages, often (though not necessarily) denoting a diminutive.
Czech, moreover, has two basic lexemes for the concept 'plum':
slíva (with a diminutive form *slíƀka*) for an 'egg plum' or 'green-
gage', and *švestka* for a 'damson'.   Most other Slavonic languages
have one basic word for all types of plum, coming from the common
Slavonic lexical root *sliva*[12] (including Slovak: *slivka*).   Exceptions involving words cognate with German *Zwetsch(g/k)e* are
Slovene, which has *češplja* (clearly coming from the Bavarian-
Austrian dialect variant /tsveʃpe/) as a synonym of *slíva,* and
Sorbian, which has *čmačka* for a 'prune' as well as *slowka* for a
'plum'.

There seems to be an etymological chicken-and-egg situation
regarding the Czech *švestka* and (Austrian-)German *Zwetschke*.
Machek (1957 : 519) states that *švestka* goes back to Old Czech
times (without citing any date), and gave rise to German *Zwetschke*.
The *Deutsches Wörterbuch* (XVI, 1105), however, supports the more
plausible thesis that the Czech word was borrowed from German.
Whichever way round the original process actually was, there would
seem to be a clear interaction between Austrian-German *Zwetschke*
and Czech *švestka*.   This is reinforced in the colloquial figurative expression *seine sieben Zwetschken* (cf. standard *Siebensachen*),

frequently associated with verbs such as *zusammenpacken*. This picturesque expression is known in Bavaria as well as Austria, and since it has no exact equivalent in standard German usage, the influence no doubt comes from the similar Czech expression *svých pět švestek* (literally meaning 'one's five damsons', and like the German used to refer to 'one's goods and chattels' or 'one's bits and pieces').

A final note on Austrian usage concerns an anomaly. The usual Austrian word for 'cottage cheese' is the Germanic lexeme *Topfen* (m.), in other words Austrian usage avoids the otherwise standard word *Quark*, which is of Slavonic origin.

III Lexical items linking usage in Austria and the GDR

Although - for reasons which will be mentioned below - the linguistic situation in the GDR is essentially different from that in Austria as far as Slavonic influences are concerned, there are a couple of items which form a geographical link between the two areas.

Schöps (m.; pl. -e), meaning a 'wether', is generally thought to come from Cz. *skopec* (with the same meaning), although, as Bielfeldt (1965 : 23) points out, Pol. *skop* or the identical Sorb. *skop* could also be a possible origin. This word is used in an eastern strip of the German-speaking area, from south east Austria up to east central Germany. It is commonly used to refer to 'mutton' in compounds such as *Schöpsenfleisch* and *-braten*. Moreover, an adjective, *schöpsern*, is derived from it, which in turn gives rise to the Austrian adjectival noun form *Schöpsernes* according to the pattern popular for various types of meat.

Pomali is listed by Ebner (1969 : 176) as an Austrian colloquialism coming from the Czech. It may occur as an adverb, meaning 'slowly' or 'little by little', or as an exclamation meaning 'hold your horses'. Karl Kraus uses it in purely dialect contexts in *Die letzten Tage der Menschheit*, while Heimito von

Doderer employs it in a higher register in the novel *Die Dämonen* (quoted by Ebner, as above): 'Wir sind schon pomali dahingezogen.' In fact the nearest Czech form is the adjective *pomalý*, while the corresponding adverbial form is *pomalu* (used in the same sense as in German). Bielfeldt (1965 : 32f.) gives *pomale* as the basic German form, referring to its widespread occurrence in dialects and relatively rare occurrence in written sources, and suggests a multiple origin from various adjacent Slavonic languages. I have so far come across only one instance of an East German occurrence, in Manfred Bieler's novel *Maria Morzeck*:[13]

> Dann polierte ich den Durchschnitt in den anderen
> Fächern auf Hochglanz und zog pomalo die schwachen
> wieder nach.

The final vowel here is nearer to that of the Czech adverb, but is perhaps more likely to have been influenced by similar forms from other languages such as Pol. *pomalu*, Sorb. *pomalu* or Russ. *pomalu* (all with the same meaning).

IV   The German Democratic Republic

When we cast a glance at the map of relations between the GDR and Slavonic languages we find a more straightforward situation than that obtaining in Austria, including its historical connections. The adjacent areas to the east, Pomerania and Silesia, are now basically Polish-speaking, while Czech is a contiguous language on the south-eastern border. Sorbian forms a linguistic island in Lusatia and an ancient substrate throughout most of the east central German area. These three West Slavonic languages give rise to several features in adjacent German dialects, but apart from the two items mentioned in the last section, influences (even lexical items) from them on the standard language normally used in the GDR are distinctly rare.

Otherwise Slavonic influences in the GDR come through a geographically indirect though politically and ideologically direct route from the Russian of the Soviet Union. The situation

contrasts sharply in many ways with that in Austria.   The latter
has and had, both geographically and historically, very extensive
ties with various Slavonic cultures, while East Germany's ties
with Russia go back only to the time of the establishment of the
Soviet Zone of Occupation in 1945.   Austria was the political
overlord vis-à-vis the Slavonic territories in question, while the
situation is reversed between the GDR and the Soviet Union.   The
linguistic effects of Slavonic tongues on Austrian-German usage
have been almost exclusively lexical, while Russian influences on
GDR usage are much more wide-reaching.

Austria and the GDR do have one - albeit negative - aspect
in common as far as their linguistic peculiarities are concerned:
in both cases there are remarkably few lexical items of purely
Slavonic origin in everyday use in the standard language.   .

If one combs the many studies now available on the peculiarities of the language of the GDR, one comes across no more than a
mere handful of Slavonic lexical items which are used to refer to
conditions in East Germany.   The vast majority of Slavonic terms
listed can be classed as exoticisms, in that, although in common
usage in the GDR press, they are normally only used to refer to
conditions in the USSR.   It is significant that a recent West
German publication by Kinne and Strube-Edelmann (1980), albeit
highly selective, lists only one word of purely Slavonic origin
(*Subbotnik*).   Comprehensive West German monographs by Reich (1968)
and Lehmann (1972) contain only four and three such words respectively, while the East German Heller's work on words of foreign
origin in contemporary German (1966) includes no Russian words of
Slavonic origin at all other than exoticisms.

The word *Subbotnik* (m.; pl. -s) is listed in practically all
relevant sources (though it is surprisingly missing from recent
editions of the Mannheim Duden and Wahrig).   The definition given
in the Leipzig Duden (1981) is:

freiwillige kollektive Arbeit sozialist.   Werktätiger
ohne Entgelt

This is usually done at the weekend, hence the derivation of the

Russian model *subbotnik* (in the same sense) from *subbota,* meaning
'Saturday'.   An occurrence in Hermann Kant's novel *Die Aula* rein-
forces the definition:[14]

> ' ... und drittens paßt das quasi nicht zu einem Subbotnik.'
>
> 'Du, Robert', rief Trullesand, 'weißt du, was er sagt?
> Er sagt wir machen hier ein[15] Subbotnik.'
>
> Robert nahm den Ton auf: 'So, sagt er das?   Was ist denn
> das, ein Subbotnik?'
>
> 'Ein Subbotnik', sagte Quasi, 'das ist eine Keimform des
> Kommunismus, ein freiwilliger Arbeitseinsatz.   Subbotnik
> kommt von Subbota, und Subbota ist russisch Sonnabend.'

The context would indicate that at the time in which the story is
set (early 1950s) the term had not yet become common parlance, but
usage has spread considerably since.   Skalická (1977) reports
that it occurs frequently in the GDR press.   A considerable number
of compounds have been recorded, e.g. *Subbotnikmittel, -stunde;
FDJ-, Jugend-, Solidaritätssubbotnik.*

Another word with the same Slavonic suffix is *Natschalnik*
(m.;   pl. *-s*), meaning 'boss', coming from Russ. *načal'nik* (with
the same meaning).   Some early studies listed this word as being
used in the GDR, but it does not seem to have caught on in popular
parlance.   A recent study by Hengst (1980 : 200) implies that
although commonly known, it is used only in specialised contexts
(presumably referring to conditions in the USSR).

The above two words have undergone opposite fates in the
Leipzig Duden.   The 1965 edition contained *Natschalnik,* but not
Subbotnik;   in the 1981 edition the position is reversed.

The Russian word *kolchoz* (a 'stump-compound' consisting of
abbreviated forms of the adjective *kollektivnoe* + the noun *choz-
jajstvo*) gives rise to a number of variant forms in German usage.
The nearest to the Russian is *der Kolchos* (except that it is often
stressed on the first syllable);   probably the commonest is *die
Kolchose* (stressed on the second syllable); *das Kolchos,* for its
part, is a rare variant (noted in Wahrig 1980, but neither in
Leipzig Duden 1981 nor Mannheim Duden 1980).   Further complications occur with the stress of the disyllabic form, in that the

Leipzig Duden allows the stress on either syllable, while the Mannheim Duden and Wahrig note it on the first syllable only.[16] Skalická (1977 : 154) suggests that the feminine form may have arisen by analogy with the semantically related *Wirtschaft* (a literal rendering of the full Russian phrase into German is *Kollektivwirtschaft*, which is indeed occasionally used in this sense). It seems to me more likely that existing German *Fremdwörter* with similar endings (e.g. *Psychose, Aprikose*) might have provided a stronger analogy in this instance.

Many authorities in both East and West refer to this word as an exoticism in German usage (e.g. Heller 1966 : 47); Lehmann 1972 : 264f.), which is certainly the case in official contexts. In colloquial contexts, however, there is evidence of its being used to refer to conditions in the GDR, invariably with a pejorative or jocular connotation. When in the GDR some years ago, I noted the statement *er arbeitet auf der Kolchose* in a context which seemed to mean no more than ... *auf dem Lande*. Ulrich Plenzdorf uses the term in striking fashion in his novel *Die neuen Leiden des jungen W.*; here it forms a distinctive element in the idiosyncratic jargon of his hero, Edgar Wibeau, who sometimes the connotation to refer to his 'empire', e.g.[17]

> Aber es soll keiner denken, ich hatte vor, ewig auf meiner Kolchose zu hocken und das.

It is interesting to note that although the idea and the institution of the collective farm was imported into the GDR from the Soviet Union, the official (and usual) expression for the East German institution - *landwirtschaftliche Produktionsgenossenschaft (LPG)* - does not have a Russian model.

Another word of Slavonic origin which is not to be found in most of the monographs on and glossaries of East German vocabulary, yet which is mentioned in other sources as being in common parlance, is *Datsche* (f.). The word comes from Russ. *dača*, meaning 'country house, holiday home'. The original Russian form *Datscha* (pl. -s) is known in German (cf. Skalická 1977 : 167), but the usual form shows phonological and morphological assimilation:

Datsche (pl. *-n*) (cf. Hengst 1980 : 203); the latter is the only
form listed in the Leipzig Duden.   Standard West German reference
works include the word in a fashion which implies that it is
largely an exoticism, e.g. 'russ. Holzhaus' (Mannheim Duden 1980),
'russ. Landhaus' (Wahrig 1980).   However, the Leipzig Duden (1981)
implies semantic assimilation by simply giving 'Landhaus, Wochen-
endhaus' as the meaning, and the West German journalist Heinrich
Brussiek (1979 : 134) cites this as the most frequently used Russian word in contemporary GDR usage.[18]   It also gives rise to a
number of compounds, e.g. *Datschenbesitzer, -grundstück, -siedlung.*

Apart from the few direct lexical loans of purely Slavonic
origin, many other Russian influences are visible in GDR German
which affect the fields of lexis, semantics and syntax.   Most of
these influences have been dealt with at length elsewhere, but I
should like to refer in summary fashion to the most striking of
such phenomena and to draw attention to certain peculiarities and
problematic aspects.

Direct lexical loans from Russian in fact embrace many more
items than the handful mentioned above, but the vast majority
of words from Russian coming into GDR German usage are words of
foreign origin in Russian.   Most are made up of components from
the classical European languages and have an international feel
to them, e.g. *Aktiv* or *Kombinat.*   Many incorporate international
agent suffixes which are already common in German, especially *-ist*
and *-ant* (cf. Sturms 1964 : 121).   *Traktorist* (Russ. *traktorist*)
is interesting as an everyday word describing a basic and common
occupation.   Not only does it form a more compact lexical item
than the standard equivalents *Traktorfahrer* or *Traktorenführer*,
but it even contains an extra emotional connotation.   This has
been expressed thus by the East German Joachim Höppner (1964 : 146):

> Es bedeutet freilich nicht nur 'Trekkerfahrer'' schlecht-
> hin, sondern schließt zugleich den Vertreter der
> sozialistischen Technik auf dem Lande ein.

Exponat (n.) was frequently cited in early western studies
of GDR usage (e.g. Moser 1962, Riemschneider 1963, Korlén 1964,
Reich 1968).   This word, meaning an 'exhibit', comes from Russ.

eksponat (with the same meaning), and was noted in East German usage from the mid-fifties on. Lehmann (1972 : 238), referring to the late sixties, states of this word: 'neuerdings auch okk. in westdt. Zeitungen'. In the course of the 1970s *Exponat* seems to have gained so much ground that it is now in common usage in all the German-speaking countries.[19] The Mannheim Duden (1980) and Wahrig (1980) list it without any reference to the GDR, while Kimme and Strube-Edelmann (1980) conversely exclude it from their glossary of GDR terms. The word is clearly more economical than semantic equivalents such as *Ausstellungs-* or *Museumstück*.

Rather ironically, certain words from western languages have found their way into GDR usage by the roundabout route via Russian. A well-known example is *Dispatcher* (Russ. *dispetčer*), referring to a 'person regulating the flow of traffic or work processes from a central point'. The English term *dispatcher* - which is unknown in everyday British-English usage - would appear to be derived from American railway terminology. The word gives rise to German compounds such as *Dispatchersystem, -zentrale*. In a literary context, the word and its derivatives were immortalised by Uwe Johnson in his novel *Mutmassungen über Jakob* (published 1959), where the central character is a *Streckendispatcher bei der Deutschen Reichsbahn*; the term occurs in this text in all sorts of variants, including back formations such as the verb *dispatchen* (not in the Leipzig Duden) and the compounding element occurring in *Dispatchbezirk*.[20]

The English term *combine harvester* was adopted by Russian in the form of the first element alone (*kombajn*), which in turn was taken over by the East Germans in the orthographically hybrid form *Kombine* (f.). In many quarters the word has been adapted both phonologically and morphologically (pl. *-n*) to German norms, though the Leipzig Duden (1981) lists the pronunciation as in Russian and English (with silent *e*) and pl. in *-s* as the first variant. Semantically, the term has been extended to cover other complex machines with similar functions, especially in agricultural contexts (e.g. *Rübenkombine*), but also in fields such as mining (e.g. *Braunkohlenkombine*).

A word of French origin largely peculiar to GDR usage which entered German via Russian is *Dispensaire* (Russ. *dispanser*), referring to a 'clinic specialising in preventive medicine'. Both the Leipzig and Mannheim Dudens (1981 and 1980, respectively) list it only in the form of the compound *Dispensairemethode* (Wahrig (1980) does not include it at all).

One of the most everyday items amongst the lexical peculiarities of the GDR is *Plast* - an international root whose form in this instance is probably accounted for by a certain amount of Russian influence. In spite of the frequent occurrence of this word, there is a controversy over its form and gender which has been noted by both eastern and western observers. Officially the word is considered to be masculine, with the plural in *-e*; colloquially, however, many speakers treat the form *Plaste* as an indivisible concept of feminine gender. The Leipzig Duden (1965) had *Plast, der* as the basic entry, while the 1981 edition appears to make a certain concession to the commonness of the form *Plaste* by giving *Plaste, Pl* as the basic entry, followed by a reference to *Sg Plast, der*; there is, however, no mention of a feminine form. Wahrig (1970; 1980) makes a reference to GDR usage, giving masc. as the main gender, and noting fem. as colloquial; this situation is confirmed by Kinne and Strube-Edelmann (1980). Most peculiar is the entry in the Mannheim Duden (1961; 1980), in that it includes the word without any reference at all to its being a GDR peculiarity, yet a considerable number of West German informants whom I have consulted were quite unfamiliar with the word in this meaning (many could think only of the trade-names of certain well-known brands of sticking-plaster!).

In practice, then, GDR usage makes a semantic distinction between *Plast*, referring to a substance, and *Plastik*, referring to '(a) sculpture' or 'plastic surgery'. West German usage of *Plastik* embraces all these meanings, though a recently acknowledged distinction gives the word neuter gender in the sense of a substance (Mannheim Duden 1980), leaving all other meanings fem. (Wahrig (1980) does not make this distinction, however, giving fem. as the only gender for all meanings.)

Plast is used in the GDR in both formal and informal contexts. One finds, for instance, technical publications with titles such as *Kleiner Wissensspeicher Plaste* and *Plaste und Kautschuk*. There are an infinite number of compounds, in both directions, involving *Plast*, such as *Plastdose, -tüte, -produkte, -verkleidung; plast-verarbeitend; Spezial-, Weichplast*. Christa Wolf in two different-ent novels provides specimens of the colloquial variant forming a compound in the forms *Plastebehälter* and *Plastebeutel*.

Heller (1966; passim) deals with *Plast* at some length, stating:

> Einen wahren Siegeszug hat das Wort *Plast* angetreten, das *Kunststoff* in Zusammensetzungen schon fast gänzlich aus dem Felde geschlagen hat.   (63)

He lists 43 recently noted compound forms from newspapers, magazines and technical journals, refers to occasional semantic distinctions made between *Plast* and *Kunststoff*, and discusses the discrepancy in genders between official (masc.) and colloquial (fem.) usage.

Remarkably, Heller makes no reference to the origin of *Plast*, nor indeed do any other of the early studies which list the word as a GDR neologism. Perhaps it was generally assumed to be merely a shortened version of *Plastik*, though why this usage should arise in the GDR alone was not explained. A connection with Russian is in fact most likely. The Russian semantic equivalent is *plast-massa*, a stump-compound from *plastičeskaja massa* (literally meaning 'plastic mass'). There is an exact German equivalent in the word *Plastmasse*, a term of East German chemical jargon referring to an 'unformed mass of plastic material'. The one well-known source making this connection is Lehmann (1972 : 348f.)[21], who makes the somewhat contrived suggestion that the monosyllabic everyday word *Plast* arose through the necessity to make further compounds out of the technical term *Plastmasse*. I would venture to propose a simpler theory: that East German *Plast* is a straight-forward clipping of Russ. *plastmassa*.

The most widespread phenomena by way of Russian (or Soviet) linguistic influences in East German usage consist in loan

translations and loan meanings. This is not only recognised in
the West, but is also freely acknowledged in the East. A statement typical of those made by many GDR linguists is to be found
in Hengst (1980 : 197):

> Der Vorbildcharakter der Sowjetunion beim Aufbau der
> sozialistischen Gesellschaftsordnung in der DDR bewirkte
> ..., daß es in einer Reihe von Fällen auch zu Lehnüber-
> setzungen und Lehnbedeutungen nach dem Muster der Verkehrs-
> sprache der Sowjetunion, dem Russischen, kam.

Such loan translations commonly take the form of compound
nouns, e.g. *Wandzeitung* (from Russ. *stennaja gazeta* or the abbre-
viated form *stengazeta*) or *Kulturhaus* (from Russ. *dom kul'tury*).
Sometimes a whole phrase is translated, as in the honorofic titles
Held der Arbeit (Russ. *geroj truda*) and *Verdienter Lehrer des
Volkes* (Russ. *zasluzennyj učitel' naroda*).

Occasionally loan translations affect parts of speech other
than nouns and phrases based on them. These are particularly
interesting in their more subtle effect: words are produced with
purely German components which were not previously in use in German. Cases in point are the verb *überfüllen* (particularly
associated with concepts such as *Soll* and *Plan*), from Russ. *perevy-
polnit'*, and the adjective *vorfristig*, from Russ. *dosročnyj*.

As far as loan meanings are concerned, many such cases involve
new meanings coming into German under Russian influence alongside
existing meanings, but tending to predominate over the previous
usage.

As an illustration of the regimentation of life in the Soviet
bloc, many words from military parlance have come to refer to
civilian settings in Russia, and hence also in the GDR. Probably
the commonest is *Brigade* (Russ. *brigada*), which affects most working environments. The associated word *Brigadier* (Russ. *brigadir*)
is surrounded by a certain degree of mystery regarding the most
official or most usual phonology and morphology in GDR usage.
The two variants are: (1) original pronunciation (as for the
military rank) as in French (ending /je/) with pl. -s; (2) new
pronunciation as in Russian (ending /ir/) with pl. -e. Many

authoritative West German sources (e.g. Lehmann 1972; Kinne and
Strube-Edelmann 1980; Mannheim Duden 1980) indicate variant (1)
as normal and (2) as less common or even colloquial.   The Leipzig
Duden (1965) gave a clear distinction in usage; (1) in military
parlance; (2) referring to the Socialist economy.   This distinction seems the most plausible, and has also been recorded by
other West German sources such as Sturms (1964 : 120) and Wahrig
(1970; 1980).   However, a more recent edition of the Leipzig
Duden clouds the issue by giving both /ir/ or /je/ as possible
variants in the meaning referring to the economy, as well as /je/
alone in a military context.   If in doubt, one always has the
form *Brigadeleiter* available to use instead!

Apart from the Russian influence, the precedent of words with
similar /ir/ endings in German usage such as *Offizier* and *Pionier*
(q.v. below), which surely occur more frequently than those with
the French pronunciation of the ending (e.g. *Portier, Bankier*),
would militate for adoption of that variant as the standard one
in the GDR.   The existence of a feminine form *Brigadierin* rein-
forces the point.   Specimens found in literary contexts (Werner
Bräunig, Christa Wolf) also show the plural form *Brigadiere*.

Other examples of extended loan meanings from (originally)
military terminology are *Pionier* (Russ. *pioner*), referring to a
member of the eponymous youth organisation, and *Kader* (Russ. *kadry*
- a plural form), referring to '(member of) qualified staff', often
with the idea of an 'elite' (by virtue of education, training or
position).   This extension of the original meaning has come to be
used in certain western circles, originally perhaps through its
use in left-wing organisations.   Both these words in their new
meanings lend themselves to a considerable number of compounds in
East German usage.

The Russian word *družba* (meaning 'friendship') has given rise
to two peculiar semantic extensions (in one case with syntactical
implications) to the basic German word *Freundschaft*.   On the one
hand, it is used to describe the less abstract concept of a unit
of the youth organisation, the *Thälmann-Pioniere*.   On the other,

it is used as a standard greeting between members of the *Freie Deutsche Jugend*. Hermann Kant reflects this usage in a humorous context in his novel *Die Aula*:[22]

> Ich kann mir keinen Körperteil denken, zu dem sie nicht 'Freundschaft, Jugendfreund!' sagen würde.

Apart from the Russian influences on lexis and semantics in the German of the GDR, one even finds considerable evidence of syntactical peculiarities attributable to Russian. This is a particularly striking phenomenon in that it affects a more funda- mental linguistic area: the very structure of the German language as used in the East German state is being eroded in many respects under Russian influence. It is hardly surprising to come across such cases in the common instances of translations of Russian speeches or writings published in the GDR press. What is more significant is to find many instances in official terminology relating to the GDR itself. The adoption of Russian models in nomenclature is especially common when the institution in question is introduced according to the Soviet pattern, though some GDR terms refer to fairly basic concepts whose nature is hardly dis- similar to parallel institutions in the western German-speaking countries. Two syntactic patterns typical of Russian and less usual in German have been frequently noted as characterising many constructions in GDR usage, which in standard German usage would be more likely to be expressed in the form of a compound noun: (a) a noun preceded by an attributive adjective (cf. Kraft 1968); (b) a noun followed by another noun in the genitive.

An example of the former pattern is the term *pädagogischer Rat*, based on Russ. *pedagogičeskij sovet* (which also occurs in the abbreviated form *pedsovet*). The institution in question hardly differs from the traditional *Lehrerkonvent*, except that apart from embracing all the teachers of a school, the GDR version also includes the Pioneer leader, a parents' representa- tive and a representative of the school's *Patenbetrieb*. The syntactic pattern of the term is reminiscent of certain ranks or titles used in the West (e.g. *Akademischer Rat, Geistlicher Rat*), rather than institutions.

The second pattern is illustrated by a set of un-German-sounding terms for basic institutions, also involving the word *Rat* and referring to executive organs of local government: *Rat der Gemeinde, Rat der Stadt, Rat des Kreises, Rat des Bezirks*. Such long drawn-out constructions involving the genitive are atypical of the syntactical pattern of German institutional terminology, where compounding is usual. The forms *Gemeinderat* and *Stadtrat* are established in most other parts of the German-speaking area; there appears to be no analogous institution in common practice attached to the administrative units *Kreis* and *Bezirk* in the West, though a partial analogy can be seen in the *Kantonsrat* of certain Swiss cantons.

In this instance Russian does not form a direct linguistic model, as the corresponding terms in fact consist of attributive adjective + noun (in most cases with an abbreviated stump-compound form in common use, e.g. *gorodskoj sovet/gorsovet*). The reason for the adoption of these unusual constructions in GDR parlance is not clear; perhaps the set of titles was deliberately reshaped in order to indicate the different ethos of the East German institutions from that of their western counterparts. It also seems possible that, although in this instance the Russian pattern did not provide the example, a certain subliminal influence of standard Russian syntax was present. Whatever the origin of these titles, they are all well established, not only in official usage but also in everyday parlance. This is evidenced by their frequent occurrence in fictional writings by GDR authors, e.g. *Rat der Gemeinde, Rat der Stadt* – Christa Wolf; *Rat des Kreises, Rat des Bezirks* – Erwin Strittmatter.

There is in fact a discrepancy in usage once the administrative hierarchy is continued upwards from the level of the *Bezirk*. At the highest level we have the *Staatsrat* – the term having the form of a more usual German compound expression (cf. *Bundesrat* – with its varying functions - in West Germany, Austria and Switzerland); this institution has no analogy in the Soviet Union. To complicate the issue further, the Russian equivalent of another important organ of government, the *Ministerrat,* is *sovet ministrov*

(literally = 'council of ministers') - in other words the pattern
of syntactic relationships is reversed from that between *Rat der
Stadt* and *gorodskoj sovet*!

Many honorific titles granted by the State are modelled
closely on Russian usage; as such they veer away considerably
from traditional German syntactic patterns and have a distinctly
clumsy and long-winded sound. The title *Verdienter Lehrer des
Volkes* was mentioned above, and many others have a similar construction involving both an attributive adjective preceding the
central noun and a further noun in the genitive following. Kinne
and Strube-Edelmann (1980 : 205) note that about 30 titles consisting of *Verdienter* + an occupation are in use. A parallel set
of titles exists with the adjective *hervorragend* (e.g. *Hervorrag-
nder Künstler des Volkes*). In this instance there is no semantic
equivalent in Russian usage, but Kraft (1968 : 76) notes that
hervorragend is a favoured epithet in the official party jargon
of the GDR, while the syntactic pattern is identical to that of
titles with *Verdienter*. Sturms (1964 : 126) suggests *das revolu-
tionäre Pathos* as a reason for the popularity of such constructions
in honorific titles.

A title awarded to successful working units is *Brigade der
sozialistischen Arbeit*, which is modelled on the Russian equivalent: *brigada kommunistiĉeskogo truda* (the GDR often uses the
epithet 'Socialist' where the USSR has 'Communist' - cf. Kraft
1968 : 76). Here the syntactical pattern is somewhat different
from that of the titles mentioned above, and although the whole
title sounds distinctly odd by western standards, its syntax is
surely acceptable by general German norms. Much less so is that
of another title with the same pattern: *Brigade der ausgezeich-
neten Qualität*, based on Russ. *brigada otliĉnogo kaĉestva*. Here
the semantics underlying the construction is different, and the
definite article is out of place (standard German usage would have
... *(von) ausgezeichneter Qualität*). We clearly have here an
instance of a mistranslation of the Russian original, arising from
the fact that Russian has no articles. Such a phenomenon would

be understandable in a nonce construction in the press, but it is astonishing that it was accepted as the wording of an official title.

Another item with less directly political undertones is the phrase *mit ... an der Spitze* based on Russ. *vo glave s ...*, which is commonly used in the GDR press as an alternative to *unter der Führung von ...* (it frequently occurs in references to delegations). This construction was listed in many early studies of East German peculiarities produced both in the West and the East. It has been so readily assimilated into German usage that in the course of the last decade or so it has crept into common use in all the western German-speaking countries as well.

Altogether three words or phrases appear to have come into fairly general German usage from Russian via the intermediary of GDR usage: *Exponat* (a *Fremdwort* of Russian), *Kader* (a loan meaning by extension of the existing one), and *mit ... an der Spitze* (a phrase based on a Russian syntactic pattern).

To conclude the section on GDR usage, I should like to refer to two particularly well-known items of GDR vocabulary which, in spite of their ideological implications, have no true Russian equivalents.   Both are compound adjectives: *volkseigen* and *kultur-voll*.   As far as *volkseigen* is concerned, the corresponding abstract noun *Volkseigentum* has a Russian equivalent in *narodnaja sobstvennost'*.   The more frequently occurring adjective, however, has no morphological equivalent in Russian; the semantic equivalent in a common collocation such as *volkseigener Betrieb,* for instance, would be *gosudarstvennyj* (= *staatlich*).   *Kulturvoll* is used to refer to the idea of 'quality of life', and occurs commonly as an adverb in the collocation with *leben*.   As such it is popular for use in many slogans, and has been listed by many observers in both West and East.   Remarkably it is not recorded in the Leipzig Duden (1965; 1981), nor in the Mannheim Duden (1980) or Wahrig (1980).   Certain East German linguistic authorities have claimed it as a loan formation from Russ. *kul'turnyj*.   This, however, does not seem fully satisfactory in that the basic meaning

of *kul'turnyj* is 'pertaining to culture', and as such has a German
equivalent in *kulturell*; a secondary meaning referring to people
would correspond more to German *kultiviert*. There is certainly
no morphological equivalent in Russian to the compound form *kultur-
voll*.

V   Conclusion

An inevitable question that poses itself is: Why are influences of Slavonic languages on German - even in Austria and the
GDR - so limited, in spite of the many geographical and historical
factors that would seem to favour them?   Orthographical peculiarities such as the Cyrillic alphabet of Russian and Ukrainian and
the unusual diacritics and consonant clusters of many other Slavonic languages are no more than a superficial hurdle.   The sound
systems of most Slavonic languages are not fundamentally dissimilar
to German, and are probably nearer in many respects to German
than that of French, which has provided so many lexical loans to
German - a good number of which retain individual sounds and sound
patterns quite foreign to German; word-order patterns are in many
ways similar to the Romance languages; word-formation conventions
may be seen to fall in between those of the Germanic and the Romance patterns.   These generalisations may produce a somewhat
dangerous oversimplification of the situation, but they are merely
intended to indicate that there are no fundamental linguistic
reasons to prevent Slavonic models from influencing German, at
least not to any lesser degree than is the case with influences
from English, French or Italian, for example.

The situation is most striking in Austria, where centuries
of extensive contact with Slavonic cultures have produced no
noticeable effect on the standard German language used in that
country other than a quite minimal number of lexical items.   In
the GDR, on the other hand, a mere couple of decades of political
contact with the Soviet Union has produced quite considerable
effects on the syntax of many common constructions (mostly with

ideological undertones) and an influx of indirect loans to the
typical vocabulary of that state (cf. Wade 1980).

It is generally recognised that the most widespread - and
most clearly visible - effect of contact between languages invariably occurs in the lexical sphere. As far as the everyday
standard language is concerned, words of purely Slavonic origin
typical of these two countries can be reduced to two items each:

Austria: *Jause* (from Slovene); *Kren* (probably from Czech)
GDR: *Datsche, Subbotnik* (both from Russian)

These contrast with the large number of direct lexical loans from
other languages - especially English, French and Italian - which
are instantly visible and audible in modern everyday German in
general, including the two countries under review. Austria, for
all its centuries of contact with Slav neighbours, has many more
words of Italian origin amongst its lexical peculiarities than
Slavonic, even though Italian-speaking territories occupied a
relatively small part of the old Austrian Empire. Moreover, a
number of studies emanating from the GDR list many more Anglo-
Americanisms as being in common use there - as in the West - than
purely Slavonic loans (cf. Heller 1966; *Geschichte der deutschen
Sprache* 1970 : 155).

The reason for the relative lack of Slavonic influences on
German in general is most likely to be of a cultural rather than
a purely linguistic nature. It quite probably stems from the
traditional lack of esteem which German-speakers had for their
Slav neighbours, whom they considered to be socially and racially
inferior. These feelings of course came to a head throughout
Germany under the Nazis, but were clearly prevalent in the old
Austrian Empire as well. If the Austrians considered the Czechs
to be at least a partially cultured nation, they tended to treat
the Slovenes, Croats, Poles, and above all the Ukrainians within
their domains as ignorant peasants. This could well account for
the one-sidedness of German-Slav linguistic contacts. It conversely could account for the relative readiness of German to
absorb French, Italian, and - especially of late - Anglo-American

linguistic influences, in that the nations in question were basically held in high regard for political and/or cultural reasons,
or underwent waves of being fashionable. Soviet Russian culture
is of course in a prestige situation in the present-day GDR, but
more through compulsion than choice. Indirect loans and *Fremdwörter* of the Russian language have slipped into German usage as
a result of the bulk of official material emanating from the USSR
and translated for East German consumption, yet the German language
- even in the GDR - remains largely resistant to absorbing purely
Slavonic lexical roots.

Acknowledgements

        I am grateful to the following colleagues in the Department
of Modern Languages at Strathclyde University for their helpful
information: Diethard Suntinger *re* Austrian usage, Dr. Terence
Wade *re* Russian, Nijole White *re* Polish, Jekaterina Young *re*
Czech; also to Dr. Ljubo Sirc of Glasgow University *re* Slovene.

Footnotes

1   Nowadays many authorities regard this language (also known as
    Cassubian) as a dialect of Polish.

2   It is only unfortunate that this invaluable work is not avail-
    able in a more accessible form.

3   All other examples given of Sorbian will be taken from Upper
    Sorbian usage.

4   Surprisingly, Bielfeldt (1965 : 44) gives no justification
    for citing only Upper Sorbian *bič* as the origin for *Peitsche*.
    In fact, the Czech, Sorbian and Polish forms have an identical
    pronunciation.

5   The modern Polish word *jucha*, of presumably the same origin
    as the Sorbian, means 'animal's blood'.

6   The same goes for Hungarian influences on Austrian German.

7   Nevertheless, the common German compound *Hagenbuttentee* is also the form used in Austria.

8   Slovak also has identical adjective and noun forms to Czech: *fešný* / *fešák*.

9   Of the few other words (all of foreign origin) in German ending *-ak* and referring to persons, two of the probably best known, *Kosak* and *Kulak*, are Russian, and are normally used only to refer to Russian conditions.

10   dtv edition, 1966, vol. 2, p.205.

11   dtv edition, 1975, p.76.

12   This root is used in all western and southern Slavonic languages to form the word for 'plum brandy': Cz. *slivovice*, Slovak *slivovica*, Sorb. *sliwowica*, Pol. *śliwowica*, Slovene *slivovec*, Sb.Cr. *šljivovica*. Hence the German *Sliwowitz*, and its phonologically corrupted - and possibly more common - variant *Slibowitz*.

13   dtv edition, 1972, p.46.

14   Fischer Bücherei edition, 1968, p.45.

15   This is the only case known to me of *Subbotnik* occurring in the neuter gender; all reference sources give masc. alone. A Rütten and Loening hardback edition (1969, p.64) also has the neut. form.

16   Yet a further complication affects Austrian usage. The Mannheim Duden (1980) notes that only *die Kolchose* is used in Austria, while the Leipzig Duden (1965; 1981) gives *der Kolchos* as the sole variant for Austria. The Leipzig Duden is obviously in error here, as the *Österreichisches Wörterbuch* (1979) only lists *die Kolchose* (this usage has also been comfirmed by an Austrian informant).

17   Hinstorff edition, 1973, p.48.

18   Dr. Karin McPherson of Edinburgh University, a frequent visitor to the GDR, informs me that she has often come across this word in conversation with city-dwelling East Germans, many of whom have the materialistic aim of owning a *Datsche*.

19   It is amusing to note its frequent occurrence even in relevant sources of the Principality of Liechtenstein (cf. publications of the National Museum of Liechtenstein and the State Postal Museum) - a country which is so much ideologically opposed to the GDR that its government recently withdrew a product of the Leipzig Duden-Verlag from use as a textbook at the State *Gymnasium* because of its pro-Communist propaganda content (cf. *Fachdienst Germanistik*, 1/2 1983, p.3).

20   Fischer Bücherei edition, 1962, pp.15 and 17.

21   On this detail, Lehmann confirms an assumption of mine propounded in undergraduate lectures at Strathclyde University from 1969 on.

22   Fischer Bücherei edition, 1968, p.226.

References

Bielfeldt, Hans Holm (1965) 'Die Entlehnungen aus den verschied-
   enen slavischen Sprachen im Wortschatz der neuhochdeutschen
   Schriftsprache' *Sitzungsberichte der Deutschen Akademie der
   Wissenschaften zu Berlin. Klasse für Sprachen, Literatur und
   Kunst* Jg. 1965, **Nr. 1.**

Brussiek, Heinrich (1979) *Notizen aus der DDR* Frankfurt, Fischer.

Deutsches Wörterbuch, vol. 16 (1954) Leipzig, Hirzel.

Ebner, Jakob (1969) *Wie sagt man in Österreich? Wörterbuch der
   österreichischen Besonderheiten* (Duden-Taschenbücher, Bd. 8)
   Mannheim/Vienna/Zürich, Bibliographisches Institut (2nd ed. 1980).

Geschichte der deutschen Sprache (1970) Berlin, Volk und Wissen.

Heller, Klaus (1966) *Das Fremdwort in der deutschen Sprache der
   Gegenwart* Leipzig, Bibliographisches Institut.

Hengst, Karlheinz (1980) 'Beobachtungen zu Entlehnungen aus dem
   Russischen ins Deutsche im Bereich des Fachwortschatzes'
   *Zeitschrift für Phonetik, Sprachwissenschaft und Kommuni-
   kationsforschung* 33 : 197-206.

Höppner, Joachim (1964) 'Widerspruch aus Weimar. Über die
   deutsche Sprache und die beiden deutschen Staaten' in:
   Friedrich Handt (ed.) *Deutsch - gefrorene Sprache in einem
   gefrorenem Land?* Berlin, Literarisches Colloquium.

Kinne, Michael and Strube-Edelmann, Birgit (1980) *Kleines
   Wörterbuch des DDR-Wortschatzes* Düsseldorf, Schwann.

Kluge, Friedrich (1967) *Etymologisches Wörterbuch der deutschen
   Sprache* 20th ed., revised by Walther Mitzka. Berlin, de
   Gruyter.

Korlén, Gustav (1964) 'Zur Entwicklung der deutschen Sprache
   diesseits und jenseits des Eisernen Vorhangs' in: Friedrich
   Handt (ed.) *Deutsch - gefrorene Sprache in einem gefrorenem
   Land?* Berlin, Literarisches Colloquium.

Kraft, Inge (1968) 'Zum Gebrauch des attributiven Adjektivs in
   beiden Teilen Deutschlands mit besonderer Berücksichtigung
   des russischen Spracheinflusses' *Muttersprache* 78 : 65-78.

Kretschmer, Paul (1969) *Wortgeographie der hochdeutschen Umgangs-
   sprache* 2nd ed. Göttingen, Vandenhoeck and Ruprecht. (1st
   ed. 1918).

Lehmann, Heidi (1972) *Russisch-deutsche Lehnbeziehungen im Wortschatz offizieller Wirtschaftstexte der DDR (bis 1968)*
   (Sprache der Gegenwart, Vol. 21) Düsseldorf, Schwann.

Leipzig Duden = *Der Große Duden. Wörterbuch und Leitfaden der
   deutschen Rechtschreibung* Leipzig, Bibliographisches
   Institut. (Editions consulted: 15th, 1965; 22nd., 1981)

Machek, Václav (1957) *Etymologický slovník jazyka českého a slovenského* Prague, Nakladatelství Československé Akademie Věd.

Mannheim Duden = *Duden. Rechtschreibung der deutschen Sprache und der Fremdwörter* Mannheim/Vienna/Zürich, Bibliographisches Institut. (Editions consulted: 15th., 1961; 18th., 1980)

Moser, Hugo (1962) *Sprachliche Folgen der politischen Teilung Deutschlands* (Beihefte zum *Wirkenden Wort* 3) Düsseldorf, Schwann.

Österreichisches Wörterbuch Vienna, Österreichischer Bundesverlag. (Editions consulted: 20th., n.d.; 35th., 1979)

Peters, Bernhard (1968) 'Deutsch-slawischer Lehnwortaustausch' in: Walther Mitzka (ed.) *Wortgeographie und Gesellschaft* Berlin, de Gruyter: 624-643.

Reich, Hans H. (1968) *Sprache und Politik. Untersuchungen zu Wortschatz und Wortwahl des offiziellen Sprachgebrauchs in der DDR* Munich, Hueber.

Riemschneider, Ernst G. (1963) *Veränderungen der deutschen Sprache in der sowjetisch besetzten Zone Deutschlands seit 1945* (Beihefte zum *Wirkenden Wort* 4) Düsseldorf, Schwann.

Rizzo-Baur, Hildegard (1962) *Die Besonderheiten der deutschen Schriftsprache in Österreich und in Südtirol (Duden-Beiträge, Bd. 5)* Mannheim, Bibliographisches Institut.

Seibicke, Wilfried (1972) *Wie sagt man anderswo? Landschaftliche Unterschiede im deutschen Wortgebrauch* (Duden-Taschenbücher, Bd. 15) Mannheim/Vienna/Zürich, Bibliographisches Institut.

Skalická, Cecília (1977) 'Slawische Entlehnungen in der Wortbildung der deutschen Gegenwartssprache' *Beiträge zur Geschichte der deutschen Sprache und Literatur* (Halle) 98 : 146-169.

Sturms, Edite (1964) 'Einige Bemerkungen zu den russisch-sowjetischen Einflüssen in der Sprache Mitteldeutschlands' in: Hugo Moser (ed.) *Das Aueler Protokoll. Deutsche Sprache im Spannungsfeld zwischen West und Ost* Düsseldorf, Schwann.

Taylor, A.J.P. (1964) *The Habsburg Monarchy* Harmondsworth, Penguin Books. (First published Hamish Hamilton, 1948)

Wade, T.L.B. (1980) 'Indirect loans in German and Russian' *Incorporated Linguist* 19 : 43-48.

Wahrig, Gerhard *Deutsches Wörterbuch* n.p., Mosaik Verlag. (Editions consulted: 1970; 1980)

NUCLEAR NEOLOGISMS

Michael Townson
(Department of Modern Languages, University of Aston in Birmingham)

The intention of this paper is to look at a particular instance
of the use of exoticisms or aliens in a very limited area of German.
Any theoretical implications which the paper has are not necessarily
only related directly to language borrowing.   They are theoretical
implications related to a number of other fields, particularly to
the fields of ideology and propaganda.   Although the title is
'Nuclear Neologisms', the area dealt with is in fact peripheral,
because attention will be focussed on an area of high technology
vocabularly well removed from the common core of the German language.   The texts under consideration illustrate a particular type
of technical register in the modern German of the present day German Federal Republic, but we shall start by looking at the reverse
process; at some German borrowings in English.   German borrowings
in English are to be found in a number of fields: education, (*kindergarten*); culture, (*zeitgeist*); psychology, (*angst*); and warfare,
and it is to this last militaristic field to which we shall address
ourselves.

There are some borrowings in English from World War I; such
as *strafe* and *zeppelin*.   There is predictably a fairly large number of instances from the National Socialist period and from the
Second World War.   The source here is the *Oxford Illustrated Dictionary*.   The relevant foreign words from German which one has in
English and which are evidenced in the *Oxford Illustrated Dictionary*
are connected with aspects of National Socialist Organization e.g.
Führer, Gauleiter, Gestapo, SA and *SS,* with aspects of military
activity such as *blitz, flak, panzer, Stalag, Oflag* and *V-weapons,*
which is of course a very interesting hybrid form, and *Wehrmacht*.
The types of word fall into a variety of morphological categories:
there are derivatives, compounds, abbreviations and initialisations.
The words are used either to name alien institutions or new concepts.

Although these words were taken into English as a result of a particular historical experience, some of them have assumed a wide distribution: *flak* for example. Their memory is kept alive by the regular production and screening of films and TV programmes on the era until this revelling in the memories of past glories was superseded to a certain degree by the opportunity to participate in that real war in the Falklands.

Now although military borrowings took place, and the word 'borrowing' is used in its widest possible sense, the borrowings were of alien terms and concepts propagated by an enemy, and they were isolated. Except in small sections of the British population, about whom we will learn little as most of the Government papers relating to the British League of Fascists are being held under the 100-Year Rule, there was at the time little attempt to adopt the referential framework or ideology which gave birth to the terms or in which they were embedded.

With the defeat of National Socialist Germany, with the occupation of German territory by the Allied Powers and with the influx of new concepts and values into the ideological vacuum left by denazification, an influx which was further promoted by the establishment of two German states, reflecting the ideological stances of their respective progenitors, it was to be expected that there would be a linguistic reflection of these processes. Although in the past conquerors and occupying forces have left their linguistic mark on subjugated territories, this has not always been accompanied by an acceptance of the conqueror's ideology. In Germany, however, these ideologies were accepted at least officially, and a study of linguistic borrowing from the original occupying powers in either German state must consider this aspect.

The move towards economic integration in both East and West, and the establishment of rigid systems of military alliance in both power blocs under the hegemony of the major powers, the USA and USSR, has greatly reduced the freedom of manoeuvre on the national level and any latitude that there is can only occur within pre-set limits. This applies particularly within the field of what is

- 89 -

called Defence Policy, where Clausewitz' *Konzert der europäischen Mächte* has been superseded by a rigid system of military alliances, and is handled most rigorously in the West towards the Federal Republic of Germany, the whole of whose armed forces are assigned to NATO. NATO Defence Policy is West German Defence Policy, West German Defence Policy is NATO Defence Policy, and it goes without saying that the assumptions underlying NATO Defence Policy also underline West German Defence Policy.

The history of armaments has been one of ever increasing lethality and technical sophistication - this is particularly true today in an age when the Arms Race has developed a momentum and dynamic of its own. A significant role in this development is played by the aerospace industry, and there can be no doubting United States predominance both here and in the fields of automation, and computer control in both civilian and military uses. It would, therefore, be most surprising if this predominance had not caused any linguistic spin-off and, of course, it has. Anybody who has flown in a Lufthansa *City Jet* will be aware of this.

Thus, given these various assumptions about the ideological influence of the dominant powers and the leading role of the United States in the West in various technical fields, one can postulate a number of hypotheses about the linguistic effects of this political situation, which we shall proceed to examine.

The first hypothesis is that there will be evidence of borrowings from American English in the vocabulary of military hardware. The second that similarly, and consequently, there will be evidence of American linguistic influence in the fields of military planning, tactics and strategy. And thirdly it is suggested that there will be a common ideological appraisal underlying the military language used, although here the linguistic borrowings or the influence may not be as patently overt as in the preceding two cases.

Although NATO strategy at present favours what planners term 'flexible response', translated into German as *flexible Reaktion* and views the options at its disposal as a continuum with no radical qualitative distinction between 'conventional' and 'nuclear' weapons (*konventionelle und nukleare Waffen*), this is a view which I do not share, and therefore as indicated by the title will be dealing essentially with nuclear hardware and nuclear strategy. The overall ideological assessment by NATO, which forms the subject of our third hypothesis is not, of course, essentially weapon-dependent, although here too there are elements which relate more clearly to nuclear weapons than to overall military strategy.

The topic under discussion here forms part of an interest in a slightly different field - the way in which governments sell Defence Policy to their populations, because in a democracy deterrents have to be sold in the same way that detergents are. For this reason, that we are dealing with nuclear terms, that there is an underlying interest in the way that governments sell their policies, the corpus underlying the present study is composed primarily of official West German documents and publications and statements for public consumption. The corpus comprises the *Weißbuch 1979*, *Zur Sicherheit der Bundesrepublik Deutschland und zur Entwicklung der Bundeswehr*, a booklet produced by the *Auswärtiges Amt* and the *Bundesministerium der Verteidigung* entitled *Es geht um unsere Sicherheit, Bündnis, Verteidigung, Rüstungskontrolle* (3rd edition 1982, quoted as *Sicherheit*), a leaflet from the *Bundesministerium der Verteidigung* called *Kräftevergleich NATO-Warschauer Pakt* (quoted as *Kräftevergleich*), and the official *Bundesministerium des Inneren* publication *Zivilschutz heute*, which deals with the civil defence side of the exercise.

As back-up material I have taken Dieter Lutz (1981) which contains an extensive list of abbreviations, a useful glossary and a technical discussion of the field.

The first point that strikes even the cursory observer is that a large number of the foreign borrowings or foreign terms under consideration are in the form of acronyms and abbreviations, as shown in Table 1. In the index to the *Weißbuch 1979*, for example, there are a total of 19 borrowings or aliens, 13 of them abbreviations and in the text itself there are approximately 35

TABLE 1

ABBREVIATIONS (Alien)

Es geht um unsere Sicherheit			*Weißbuch 1979*
GLOSSARY			REGISTER
ABM	MBFR	SALT	ABM (-Vertrag)
ICBM	MIRV	START	AWACS
INF	PNE	SLBM	ALCM, GLCM, SLCM
			ICBM
Text			MBFR
NATO			MIRV
SALT			LTOP
START			AMF
MBFR			TNF
MIRV			SLM
INF			SALT
LRTNF			
GLCM			Text
NPG			above and
			SLBM
			ASBM
			SRTNF, MRTNF, LRTNF
			MRBM/IRBM
			DPC

aliens, 21 of these being abbreviations. Two main reasons can be found for the preponderance of abbreviations.

The first is that the nuclear weapons debate is itself governed by acronyms and abbreviations.[1] A glance at the glossary of Lutz (1981), which gives a technical overview of the field, seems to confirm this. Lutz's list contains 145 abbreviations, 82 of which are of English origin, dealing specifically with nuclear weapons, nuclear strategy and control.

A second reason, which is perhaps of more interest for the present purpose, is that acronyms, and to a lesser extent

abbreviations, can be de-coupled from their origins, and assume
an existence as words in their own right. Examples of this from
German into English can be seen with *flak* and from English into
German with *NATO*. *NATO* is, in fact, an interesting case.   There
does not seem to be any move in German to convert this into *NAVO,*
which is what one might expect, *Nordatlantische Vertragsorganisa-*
tion; they seem content to rest with NATO, even though obviously
'Treaty' does not occur in German, whereas the so-called Warsaw
Pact or *Warschauer Pakt* is referred to variously both as WTO
(Warsaw Treaty Organisation) and WVO (*Warschauer Vertragsorgani-*
sation).   As the case of *V-weapons* demonstrated, hybrid forms
can arise by breaking the link; an instance of this in German is
given in Lutz (1981) who refers to an *RB/ER-Waffe*; the original
English is 'Reduced Blast/Enhanced Radiation Weapon', commonly
known as the Neutron Bomb (*Neutronenbombe*).   Another case in point
where an acronym has been de-coupled, is that of MIRV, which stands
for Multiple Independently Targetable Re-entry Vehicle, an interesting term in its own right, the Multiple Independently Targetable
Re-entry Vehicle - because nowhere here does the term weapon, bomb,
warhead or anything else occur.   It is an interesting 'vehicle'.
In English this acronym MIRV has become sufficiently well established to undergo morphological processes, so one finds *mirving* and
mirved and in Lutz (1981) there is an interesting instance of *ver*
mirvt, where *MIRV* is thus translated from the status of a stray
alien to that of a root morpheme.

> *Die SS-20 trägt einen vermirvten Gefechtskopf mit drei*
> *unabhängig voneinander auf drei Zielpunkte, programmier-*
> *bare* (sic) *Sprengladungen.*
>
> (Lutz 1981:151)

It is interesting that the abbreviation MIRV has been taken over
and has been used as a root of a verb, *vermirven,* but it is still
felt necessary to explain what it means.   It is a mirved warhead
'ein vermirvter Gefechtskopf'.   *Gefechtskopf* is also interesting
as a possible loan translation of 'warhead'.

    Following on from that and engaging in some speculation it
is conceivable that the naturalization processes could reach the

stage where an acronym which is homophonous with a foreign real word is erroneously identified with the real word and translated as it. An example which occurs to one here is that of a particular type of weapon known as a *Frog*. A *Frog* one could see being rendered as *Frosch* in possible ignorance of the fact that *Frog* is in fact itself an acronym. It stands for *Free Rocket Over Ground*, and thus falls into a different category from the other weapon systems which have been given animal names, such as *Bär, Bison, Jaguar, Gepard, Leopard* and the rest.

There are two stages in the de-coupling process of the abbreviation from its origin. Initially the abbreviation or acronym is related in the publications under consideration to its English origin and as close as possible a translation of this is given in German. The English term can then be dropped, so one has an English based abbreviation with a German term linked with it, there being no apparent link between the initials of the abbreviation and the initials of the German term. What can then happen, after this first de-coupling, is that the German translation is modified. This has happened very clearly in the case of TNF (Theatre Nuclear Forces) for which the original German equivalent is *Kriegsschauplatzgebundene nukleare Waffen*, as direct a translation as one can get. But this has now become referred to in official parlance as *Nuklearkräfte in und für Europa* and Lutz comments this as follows:

> *Deutlicher als der englische Ausdruck 'Theatre Nuclear Forces' weist der deutsche Begriff der 'Nuklearkräfte in und für Europa' auf die Landzielorientierung und auf den Kriegschauplatz Europa hin, für den TNF Systeme vorgesehen sind.* (Lutz 1981: 370)

So whereas the Americans on the other side of the Atlantic Ocean can call them Theatre Nuclear Forces, not meaning any theatre in particular, although they are going to be stationed in Europe, the Europeans, who are getting the things on their doorstep, tend to be a little more precise with the designation attached to these weaponry.

The next point which can be made with regard to the short forms, the abbreviations and acronyms, is a stylistic one. One can assume that the number of outright alien terms or exotics used is a measure of the esotericity of the language. In this particular case the esoteric nature of the register is equivalent to the technicality of the discussion: the more popularized the account, the fewer the technical terms used. To a certain extent the technicality of the discussion is also reflected in the length of the text concerned. If one refers to the abbreviations in Table I from *Es geht um unsere Sicherheit* and from the *Weißbuch 1979*, there are more of them in the *Weißbuch* than in the shorter publication, the *Weißbuch* having more technical discussion and thus containing a far larger number. Taking all four texts, 1) the leaflet *Kräftevergleich NATO-Warschauer Pakt*, 2) the booklet *Es geht um unsere Sicherheit*, 3) the book *Weißbuch 1979*, and 4) the technical discussion, Lutz 1981 *Weltkrieg gegen Willen*, we find a clear progression in the number   English abbreviations used.   Number one, the leaflet has 4 -   TO, ICBM, INF, SNF; number two, the booklet has 13; number three the *Weißbuch* has 20 and number four Lutz has 82 (see Table II), and this can of course be related quite clearly to the public for whom these various documents are intended.

The *Kräftevergleich* leaflet which contains principally pictures, which are much easier to understand than text, is aimed at the general public who do not really take much interest in these matters. The booklet *Es geht um unsere Sicherheit* is written for those who like to feel that they are well informed. The *Weißbuch 1979* is intended for politicians and diplomats, and Lutz (1981) is designed for those who take a more professional or concerned interest in the matters under consideration.

An examination of the referents of these abbreviations does indeed show an increase in technical detail and sophistication. None of the publications has managed to de-couple the abbreviations and their origins completely, although the leaflet *Kräftevergleich* does go furthest in this respect. The English referent for an

TABLE II

Lutz, Dieter (1981)

Abkürzungsverzeichnis

ABM	FBS	NCA	TNF
ACE	FOBS	NUP	
ADM		NSTL	WWMCCS
ALBM	GLCM		
ALCM		OAR	Y
ASM	ICBM	OBM	
ASW	IRBM		
		PK	
BM	LR		Total : 145
	LRTNF	RB	
C³			Total US/Eng : 103
CBM	MBFR	SB	
CEP	MIRV	SLBM	- non-nuclear
CM	MLF	SLCM	US proper names and
	MMIRBM	SRAM	institutions : 21
DCA	MRCA	SRBM	
	MRCM	SRM	Specific nuclear
ECM	MRTNF	SRTNF	abbreviations : 82
EMP	MRV	SSBN	
EP	MURFRAANCE	SSKP	
ERW		SSM	

Glossar:

Erstschlagfähigkeit(first-strike capability) - counterforce
Flexible Response
Gesicherte Zerstörung (assured destruction)
Letalität, Kill Capability
MBFR
SALT
TNF
Letalitätsradius
Zweischlagfähigkeit (second-strike capability) - countercity,
    countervalue

abbreviation is very often left out.   Here on the one hand we are
dealing with increasing technical detail and sophistication;   on
the other hand, and concomitantly, we have increasing simplifi-
cation and popularization;   if one is trying to put across a simple
political message, one does not wish to get bogged down in a mass
of technical detail.   And the leaflet *Kraftevergleich* is trying
to put over a simple technical message.   It is suggested that this

is in fact a feature which is common to all forms of public relations, including advertising, that the specific and technical features of a product are diluted the further the process of popularization proceeds. The addressee, or consumer, at the bottom of the scale, is confronted with conclusions presented as facts, regardless of whether it is *Berlin tut gut, Es gibt nichts Besseres als Benz Polstermöbel, Vitamin A Augenkapseln schützen die Sehkraft* or *Der Bedrohung durch den Warschauer Pakt begegnet das Bündnis mit der bewährten Strategie der flexiblen Reaktion.* All these are presenting conclusions as facts and expecting people to believe them and buy the product.

A closer analysis of the abbreviations found in the *Weißbuch 1979* shows that the aliens refer to weapon systems such as ABM (Anti-ballistic missile), ICBM (Inter Continental Ballistic Missile), MIRV, to weapons plus their uses (as in TNF), to planning groups (LTDP - Long Term Defence Planning, and DPC - Defence Planning Committee) to Arms Control agreements and negotiations (MBFR and SALT). The weapons thus labelled are of American origin, the strategies or plans are either United States or NATO creations (and English is after all the language of NATO) and the Arms Control Agreements and Negotiations are ones in which either the United States of America was the sole NATO member involved (as with SALT and START), or plays a leading role as in the Vienna MBFR (Mutually Balanced Force Reduction Talks).

In the sphere of conventional weapons and in matters of internal Bundeswehr organization, one does of course find more German based short forms and the same applies to international negotiations in which the Federal Republic of Germany is engaged as a participant in its own right., as in KSZE for example.

Before proceeding to consider the alien 'full terms', i.e. not the abbreviations, in German, it is perhaps worth mentioning a small group of English names which occur in the *Weißbuch 1979,* and these are names given to both military exercises (for example REFORGER) and weapons systems (BACKFIRE, LANCE, MINUTEMAN, PERSHING, POLARIS, TRIDENT, TITAN, TOMAHAWK, and TORNADO); two of these are neutral as to origin - TITAN, TORNADO, although within their context they are not likely to be specifically German, although the TORNADO as a joint European project is in a somewhat ambivalent position. The others all refer to US systems with the exception of BACKFIRE which is in fact a common NATO code-name for a new Soviet bomber.

So far we have dealt with initializations and proper names and we can now proceed to the full terms and as already indicated, these are not as numerous as the initializations and in fact some· of them are co-referential with the initializations.

TABLE III

TERMS (ALIEN)

Es geht um unsere Sicherheit	*Weißbuch 1979*
Intermediate Range Nuclear Forces 1)	**Register**

Register

Common collective ceiling (MBFR)
Cruise Missile
Defence Planning Committee
High Level Group/Special Group
Rapid Reinforcement Concept
UN Peace Keeping Operations

Text   above and

First Strike Capability
Second Strike Capability
Air Launched Cruise Missile
Sea Launched Missile
Theater Nuclear Forces
(Short Range, Medium Range, Long Range)

+ Names of Exercises and Weapons

REFORGER	MINUTEMAN	TRIDENT
BACKFIRE	PERSHING	(TITAN)
(JAGUAR)	POLARIS	(TOMAHAWK)
LANCE		

At first sight there would appear to be very few such terms and they do not all appear particularly nuclear-specific, particularly such terms as 'Common Collective Ceiling'. However, the terms that do occur in the text both of *Es geht um unsere Sicherheit* and the *Weißbuch 1979* are of crucial importance to the nuclear weapons debate in general and the European debate in particular.

That the English terms used are not restricted to the specifically military field is shown by an example of a hybrid from the FRG Civil Defence Publication *Zivilschutz heute, für den Bürger, mit dem Bürger*; under the section *Aufenthaltsregelung* (one might think that *Aufenthaltsregelung* is a type of residence permit for visitors to Germany). In fact, *Aufenthaltsregelung* refers to plans for the civilian population when the bomb drops. One reads here:

> *In einem Verteidigungsfall bedeutet Flucht Vergrößerung der Gefahr ... Um die Gefährdung zu mindern, hat die NATO den Grundsatz des Zuhausebleibens aufgestellt. Diese sogenannte Stay-Put-'Bleib wo du bist' Politik ist eine der Voraussetzungen für das Überleben der Menschen.*
> *(Zivilschutz: 50)*

There are interesting assumptions and presuppositions here, that survival is possible and that staying at home will increase one's chances of survival. Here again we are dealing with official NATO policy and therefore, preference is accorded to the English term (although in fact we are dealing with a highly complex hybrid, as the orthography shows, where interestingly it is the *German* element which is placed in inverted commas).

A potentially more fruitful and at the same time more problematical line of investigation is revealed, however, if the terms of reference are widened to include not only these loan words, but also loan translations. The line is more fruitful in that it widens the scope of the investigation, but more problematical in that one is moving very rapidly from an investigation of expression to a study of content, which causes a number of methodological problems. As we have seen, the existence of a possible loan translation indicates that a concept might have become naturalised, but

- 99 -

the pedigree is often difficult to follow, and the existence of
translation equivalents does not necessarily point to linguistic
borrowing. Thus although *gesicherte Zerstörung* is a translation
equivalent of 'assured destruction' the borrowing is probably con-
ceptual rather than linguistic. (It is incidentally interesting
to see that German does not have the equivalent of the English and
American 'mutual assured destruction', which is usually abbreviated
as MAD; *Gegenseitige gesicherte Zerstörung* does not have quite
the same effect.) The problem becomes even more intractable when
one starts considering the mechanisms of language manipulation for
control purposes. Here one can definitely point to parallels
between English and American on the one hand and German on the
other, but the devices used, such as euphemism and playing down
of danger and presentation of threat are probably universal, albeit
with language specific manifestations, and possibly ideology-
specific realizations.

TABLE IV

Weißbuch 1979 (Text)   *Es geht um unsere Sicherheit*
                                                         (Text)

nuklear-strategische Waffensysteme	Nuklearwaffen
ballistische Raketen	NATO-Trade (dreischichtiges
Parität, nukleare Balance	Waffenspektrum)
strategische Nuklear-Uboote	Abschreckungsspektrum
Cruise Missiles	konventionelle Kräfte
Marschflugkörper	Rüstungskontrolle (cf.KRSt)
Wurfgewicht	Offensivsysteme
Nuklearbomben	Verifikation (cf.Nachprüfbar-
nukleare Kräfte, Nuklearkräfte	keit)
nuklearfähige Jagdbomber	Bodenluftflugkörper
Eskalationsspektrum	Null-Lösung

One indication for a loan translation is the choice of a word
itself of foreign origin in the host language, particularly if
this word has a phonological or morphological similarity to the
borrowed term. An example of this would be the use of *Parität*
and *Nukleare Balance* to render 'Parity' and 'Nuclear Balance'.
Along with these terms one also finds the use of *Gleichgewicht*
which is a term of long-standing in politics and diplomacy.

However, *Gleichgewicht, Gleichgewichtspolitik, Ausgleichspolitik*
is for the historian, at least, linked more with the concept of
'Balance of Power' which has undergone a transformation with the
advent of the major power bloc dominated nuclear age.   So there
is a tendency in the publications under consideration to use terms
like *Balance* and *Parität* rather than the 'German' term *Gleichgewicht*.

Another example is to be found in use of *Spektrum* which occurs
in a number of compounds such as *Eskalationsspektrum* and *Abschreckungsspektrum*.   'Spectrum' is a term much beloved of the Pentagon
and one would be justified in seeing some linguistic influences
here between the Pentagon 'spectrum' and the use of *Spektrum* in
Abschreckungsspektrum and *Eskalationsspektrum*.   A further indication of borrowing in the form of loan translation can be found in
the case of compounds which follow the morphology of a presumed
origin exactly.   A clear instance of this is to be found with the
term *Wurfgewicht* which is a direct translation of the English 'throw-weight', designating the pay-load of a nuclear vehicle.   The
formulation of *Wurfgewicht* is unnecessary, as there is a perfectly
good German term available in the form of *Nutzlast*.   Incidentally,
'throw-weight' is also redundant, as the term 'pay-load' already
exists, but 'pay-load' seems to be restricted more to peaceful
rockets, like space shuttles and moon probes and such like.

The mention of 'throw-weight' and *Wurfgewicht* leads on to the
problem for German of dealing with the English term 'missile'.
'Missile in English covers both ballistic and guided missiles, regardless of the propulsion system, guided missiles including the
subcategory of cruise missiles.   German does not have one term with
the same range of reference.   *Wurfgeschoß*, apart from being slightly archaic, precludes guided missile, as too should another common
dictionary equivalent *Rakete*.   Rockets are rather old-fashioned
in English, or else the term is often restricted to a particular
type of propulsion system of a space craft of missile.   In military terms one talks about ballistic missiles rather than rockets.
A rocket or a *Rakete* is a ballistic projectile.   None the less,
German military language uses the term *ballistische Rakete* which

is somewhat tautological, *Rakete ist ballistisch*, as there is no corresponding *gelenkte Rakete* so what they have tried to do is to translate 'missile' with *Rakete* but have also kept the redundant *ballistisch* with it. For 'guided missiles' German either has to use *Munition* as in the case of PGM (*Präzisionsgelenkte Munition* - 'Precision Guided Munitions*), itself an interesting example of a German term being constructed to match the English abbreviation PGM, or the generic term *Waffen* with its compound *Lenkwaffe*, or the term *Flugkörper*, which is found in *Marschflugkörper*, of which more later, and of which the Navy seems particularly fond. It is incidentally interesting to see the difference in linguistic use between the arms of the *Bundeswehr* - the Navy prefers *Flugkörper*. For example :

> *Die Marinefliegergeschwader werden mit weitreichenden Flugkörpern gegen Schiffsziele ausgestattet* and *10 Flugkörperschnellboote* (i.e. a guided missile destroyer or patrol boat) *der Klasse 143A werden beschafft. Sie werden mit Flugkörpern sowohl gegen See-Ziele als auch zur Flugabwehr ausgestattet sein.*
>
> (*Weißbuch*: 176)

So the Navy prefers *Flugkörper*; the Army and Air Force seem fonder of *Flugabwehrraketen*, rather than *Flugabwehrkörper*.

While dealing with the terms central to the discussion as 'missile', it might be opportune to consider the most central term of all - 'Nuclear'. It is interesting to observe here that although German has the possibility of compounding with *Kern* - and does indeed with *Kernwaffen* and *Kernkraft*, *Kernforschung*, *Kernspaltung*, *Kernfusion*, there is an almost complete absence of compounds with *Kern* in the corpus under investigation. The index of *Weißbuch 1979*, for example, instances only one case and that is the concept of *Kernwaffenteststop*, an interesting one : the *Es geht um unsere Sicherheit* book does not talk about them.

Preference is accorded to the double foreigner *nuklear*, *Nuklear-*, which can be used either as an independent attributive adjective *nukleare Waffen* or as a compounding element e.g. *Nuklearkräfte*. It is suggested that what is happening here is that the term *Nuklear-* is being restricted to a military use, whereas in the wider context, *Kern-* is still used as in *Kernkraft* for example.

It would perhaps be going too far to suggest that in those areas in which the Federal Republic itself is actively involved e.g. nuclear power, there is a tendency to use *Kern-* whereas in other cases *Nuklear-* is used.   It is still interesting to note that in the Appendix 6 to *Es geht um unsere Sicherheit* there is a survey of multilateral and bi-lateral arms control agreements.   *Multilaterale Rüstungsbegrenzungsabkommen 1925 bis 1979* and *Bi-laterale Rüstungsbegrenzungs- und Rüstungskontrollabkommen USA/Soviet Union ab 1963,* and that in the summary of every nuclear agreement to which the Federal Republic of Germany is a signatory, the term *Kernwaffen* is used, whereas in all the others to which the Federal Republic is not a signatory, the terms used are either *Nuklearwaffen* or the more neutral *Atomwaffen.*

Nuklear- is not limited to an element in nominal compounds; one also finds adjectival compounds such as *nuklearstrategisch* and *nuklearfähig,* as in *Nuklearfähige Jagdbomber,* which are 'Strike attack aircraft with nuclear capability'.

Mention of capability leads one to a consideration of the terms 'First Strike Capability' and 'Second Strike Capability' in the corpus.   In this corpus, these terms are used both in the original English and in loan translation: *Erstschlagfähigkeit und Zweitschlagfähigkeit.*   In the *Weißbuch 1979,* the loan translations are given priority and only they, and not the English terms occur in the index.   In the *Weißbuch 1979* the terms are explained in general terms as follows:

First Strike:

> *ein entwaffender Erstschlag, der das gesamte nuklearstratigische Langstreckenpotential der anderen Seite ausschalten kann.*

And a Second Strike:

> *ein Zweitschlag, eine Antwort auf einen nuklearen Angriff.*
> (*Weißbuch*:99)

If the discussion becomes more detailed, and thus technically more explicit, as it does in Lutz (1981), recourse is then had to specialised terms from English which do not appear to have specific one word equivalents in German. These terms being 'counterforce' (for the first strike capability) and 'countercity' and 'countervalue' for Second Strike Capability. These terms are used as English terms in the German text.

One of the arguments over the planned deployment of nuclear weapons in Western Europe is whether these weapons have a first or second strike capability and how they would be used. One of these weapons, the Cruise Missile, provides the final example in this section.

The details given in the *Weißbuch 1979* of the Cruise Missile are interesting for a variety of reasons, not all of them linguistic. (For example why does the *Weißbuch* not mention GLCM even though it was published only 3 months before the now famous NATO dual/twin track decision ?) (*Doppelbeschluß*)
We read:

> *Die Cruise Missiles sind im Prinzip keine neuen Waffen.*
> *Marschflugkörper gibt es schon lange.*
> (*Weißbuch*: 103)

We find the English and German terms being used in adjacent sentences: *Cruise Missiles sind im Prinzip keine neuen Waffen. Marschflugkörper gibt es schon lange.* It is suggested that there is some difference in reference between them, in that 'Cruise Missile' is taken to have specific reference to a new generation of U.S. weapons, whereas the *Marschflugkörper* has generic reference, as becomes clear in the wider context of the quotation. Thus the German term is the generic term, while the English is kept for the specific and thus assumes some of the characteristics perhaps of a proper name.

The interesting question however is where the term *Marschflugkörper* comes from, and how the analysis of the compound is to be carried out. Given the previous remarks about the translation of missile, one would expect *Marsch/flugkörper*. Some technical aeronautical dictionaries contain the term *Marschflug* for what is commonly referred to as *Reisefluggeschwindigkeit*, 'cruising speed' and *Marschflug* seems to owe its origin to the nautical *Marschfahrt*, which is a ship's cruising speed, so that from this we would appear to have a *Marschflug/körper* which is a loan translation for the cruise missile. The actual analysis, though, is probably *Marschflug-Flugkörper*, with one of the *Flug*-elements being deleted.

From the discussion up to this point which has been primarily technical in orientation, i.e. technical in both the military and the linguistic sense, there would appear to be sufficient evidence to justify both our first hypothesis, that there will be borrowings from English in the vocabulary of military hardware, and our second hypothesis that, similarly and consequently, there will be evidence of American linguistic influence in the fields of planning, tactics and strategy. The evidence for this influence is to be found both in direct borrowings and in loan translations, whereby the direct borrowings are to be found in proper names, short forms (acronyms and abbreviations) and in full terms.

As has already been indicated, the third hypothesis, that there will be a linguistic reflection of the common ideological appraisal underlying the military appraisal, is a far more difficult one to come to grips with, as we are entering the area of content rather than expression. The question is far more problematic, in that one must look at the textual organisation rather than individual items of lexis, and it is uncertain to what extent the mechanisms involved are general rather than specific. There is, for example, the way the military establishment is referred to as 'defence', *Verteidigung* even though its strategy is based mainly on offensive weapons, and the way in which the possession of these offensive weapons is justified in the interests of 'deterrence', *Abschreckung*. These are features which one will find in both major power blocs. There is also the concept of 'threat', *Bedrohung* which underlies military thinking. The presentation of a real, perceived or fictitious threat is probably a stratagem used by the military throughout the world to justify the demands for increased

military expenditure.   And it is interesting that Cruise Missiles
are presented in one British Defence Ministry publication as the
West's life insurance.   People can only be sold life insurance if
they think their life is under threat, in some way.

A full consideration of the ideological assumptions underlying
the discourse of official West German defence publications would
transcend the bounds of the present paper, so we shall restrict
ourselves to running very quickly through a few of the basic assumptions which can be set up, the basic ideological assumptions,
and which one finds throughout official government writings on Defence Strategy in English (both American and British) and German.

The first one is that nuclear weapons are a necessary fact of
life and are forces for the good, in that they protect the superior
values of the West.   They are necessary facts of life and are not
intrinsically bad things so we find evidence here of euphenism,
for example in the way that terms such as 'weapons' and 'bombs'
are avoided in favour of terms such as 'systems' or 'potential'

The second one is that there is a threat from the Soviet Union,
from the Warsaw Pact.   (*Der Bedrohung durch den Warschauer Pakt
begegnet das Bündnis...*)

The third one is that nuclear weapons are necessary to preserve
peace - *Die bewährte Strategie der flexiblen Reaktion*, i.e. peace
has only been preserved because the USSR has been deterred from its
aggressive intentions by NATO's nuclear weapons, it is a *bewährte
Strategie*.

The fourth is a danger of the USSR gaining an overwhelming nuclear superiority which is why one has to produce evidence of *Kräftevergleich* and *Kräfteüberlegenheit*.

Fifthly that governments are the only true peace movements -
others are either misguided, playing into the hands of the enemy,
or in his service.   It is interesting to see the way that peace
movements in Britain, in the Federal Republic, and to a very great
extent in the GDR, are regarded as dissident, anti-establishment,
endangering elements, and it also interesting to see that, although

in the Western democracies we have freedom of speech, and we can
protest, whose who do protest are still classed as opponents of the
status quo, and thus as disruptive as potentially dangerous elements.
They are allowed to protest, but their protest is of no avail.
There is an interesting quote from Chomsky, although this is not
one of his technical books on linguistics:

> *A totalitarian stage simply enunciates official doctrine.*
> *In a democratic system of propaganda, no one is punished*
> *for objecting to official dogma, in fact dissidence is*
> *encouraged. What the system attempts to do is to fix*
> *the limits of possible thought, supporting the official*
> *doctrine at one end and the critics at the other. No*
> *doubt a propaganda system is more effective when its*
> *doctrines are insinuated rather than asserted, when it*
> *sets the bounds of possible thought, rather than simply*
> *imposing a clearly and easily identifiable doctrine that*
> *one must parrot.*
>
> (Chomsky 1979:20)

The above features are all to be found in the corpus under consideration, and they form parallels to official American and British
defence publications. They are parallels caused by common assumptions and a common perception of the geopolitical situations; it
would be a mistake to regard them as being imposed on the FRG, but
on the other hand one should have no illusions about where the
dominant culture and power in the Western Alliance lies.

Another presupposition is that if a nuclear war does break
out, it is winnable and controllable. One finds references to
*das Überleben der Bevölkerung, die flexible Reaktion, das Eskala-
tionsspektrum,* all this as though we are dealing with logical categories which were controllable, which were rational, and which can
be switched on or off at will to suit particular circumstances.

It is on this final point that one might be permitted to have
one's strongest doubts.

Footnotes

1   cf. Smith, D (1980) 'The subject of military policy has developed its own language; ... One feature of the language is its love of initials and acronyms.' (pp.14-15)

References

Auswärtiges Amt/Bundesministerium der Verteidigung (1982^3)
Es geht um unsere Sicherheit. Bündnis. Verteidigung. Rüstungskontrolle. Bonn.

Bundesminister des Innern (1979)   *Zivilschutz heute - für den Bürger - mit dem Bürger.* Bonn.

Bundesminister der Verteidigung (1979) *Weißbuch 1979. Zur Sicherheit der Bundesrepublik Deutschland und zur Entwicklung der Bundeswehr.* Bonn.

Bundesministerium der Verteidigung   *Kräftevergleich NATO-Warschauer Pakt.* Bonn.

Chomsky, Noam (1979)   *Language and Responsibility.* Harvester Press.

Crispin, Aubrey (ed. 1982)   *Nukespeak. The Media and the Bomb.* London, Comedia.

Lutz, Dieter S. (1981)   *Weltkrieg wider Willen? Die Nuklearwaffen in und für Europa.* Hamburg, Rowohlt.

Smith, Dan (1980)   *The Defence of the Realm in the 1980s.* London, Croom Helm.

AGAINST THE TIDE - THE INFLUENCE OF GERMAN ON ENGLISH

A.W. Stanforth
(Heriot-Watt University)

Throughout its history the German language has been subject
to strong influences from other languages. Linguistic historians
have found it possible and convenient to describe such foreign
linguistic influences in terms of successive waves: the biggest
of these to wash over German have been Latin during the Roman
occupation of the lands on the Rhine and Danube, and during the
period of conversion to Christianity; French during the Middle
Ages; Latin again during the Renaissance; French in the seventeenth and eighteenth centuries; English during the nineteenth
and twentieth centuries, with American English (AE) taking over
from British English (BE) after the Second World War.

Intense linguistic influence can provoke equally intense
puristic sentiment; in the case of German we can point to the
efforts of the *Sprachgesellschaften* during the Frenchified
à-la-mode period, and of the *Allgemeiner deutscher Sprachverein*
in the period leading up to the First World War and again in the
1930s. Since 1945 concern has occasionally been expressed at
the massive influx of Anglicisms, but by and large the subject
has been dealt with within academe, in contexts such as the
present one, with appropriate scholarly restraint. In recent
years German scholars have tended more and more to view the
phenomenon of borrowing in a wider context: the realisation has
grown that: i) nearly all languages borrow from each other;
ii) English, and especially AE, is a potent influence on languages
throughout the world and not just on German; iii) the German
language itself is used outside Germany's frontiers; and
iv) German has exerted and continues to exert an influence on
other languages. In short, German treatment of the loan-word
question has become less parochial, less inward-looking, and the
subject has been reorientated within the context of the general
theme 'languages in contact'.

This may be exemplified as follows: in 1968 a *festschrift* for the then director of the *Deutscher Sprachatlas*, L.E. Schmitt, appeared with the title *Wortgeographie und Gesellschaft* (Mitzka, 1968). It contained a section - some 230 pages long - entitled 'Lehnwortaustausch des Deutschen mit den Nachbarsprachen', in which not merely the influence of French, Italian, English, Dutch, Scandinavian, Slavonic and Hungarian on German was charted, but also the impact of German on those languages. In 1977 two books appeared on the theme 'German in contact with other languages'. The first of these bore just this title; edited by Molony, Zobl and Stölting it printed the papers of a conference held at Essen the previous year (Molony *et al.*, 1977). The second, also a collection of papers, was entitled *Deutsch als Muttersprache in Kanada* (Auburger & Kloss, 1977). This was the inaugural volume of an important new series, *Deutsche Sprache in Europa und Übersee*, which at my last count had seven volumes to its credit. Two of the editors of this series, Leopold Auburger and Heinz Kloss, put out a further collection in 1979 as volume 43 of the *Forschungsberichte des Instituts für deutsche Sprache*, entitled *Deutsche Sprachkontakte in Übersee* (Auburger & Kloss, 1979), while Heinz Kloss's monumental study *Die Entwicklung neuer germanischer Kultursprachen seit 1800*, which treats the development and interaction of the Germanic family, had gone into a revised second edition the year before (Kloss, 1978). A further mammoth collection of conference papers deriving from a symposium held in 1979 by the Research Centre for Multilingualism in Brussels appeared as volume 32 of the *ZDL Beihefte* in 1980 (Nelde, 1980). The upsurge of interest in linguistic interaction in the widest sense - lexical borrowing, linguistic problems of *Gastarbeiter*, German language overseas, standard/dialect interference - led me during these years to set up a special section of the chapter on German language in *The Year's Work in Modern Language Studies*, and it became one of the fullest.

The developments I have sketched here have been mirrored in the *Entstehungsgeschichte* of our present conference: originally billed as 'Foreign Influences on German, Past and Present' the

organisers subsequently widened the focus to 'Deutsch im Kontext
der Nachbarsprachen'. By so doing they have enabled me to offer
my remarks on the influence of German on English without, myself,
swimming too blatantly, 'against the tide'.

My interest in the history of borrowing between English and
German started in the late 1960s, when I was asked to write the
chapter 'Deutsch-Englischer Lehnwortaustausch' in the *festschrift*
for L.E. Schmitt mentioned above. (The word *festschrift*, by the
way, may stand as my first example of a German loan-word in
English.) While working on it I was struck by the not insignificant contribution that German has made to the English vocabulary.
Compared with the tide running from English to German the amount
flowing in the opposite direction may seem, to use Anthony
Sampson's word (1968 : 269) 'a trickle', but nevertheless over
the years the English vocabulary has been enriched by German to
a greater extent than I had been aware. In his study of the
English lexicon Manfred Scheler (1977 : 72), relying heavily on
studies by Finkenstaedt, and Wolff (1973), has attempted to ascertain statistically the etymological origins of our wordstock.
He finds that German - and I mean here High German - accounts for
0.5% of our vocabulary. We must allow for statistical error and
other factors, such as the choice of dictionaries used to provide
the base; for instance, if the *OED* had been used instead of the
SOED, the number of Germanisms would have doubled. Nevertheless,
Scheler's figure of 0.5% is more than that given for Celtic
(0.34%), Anglo-Celtic (0.09%) and the remaining (i.e. excluding
Romance, Greek and Germanic) European languages taken together
(0.13%). On this count Germanic overall makes up 26.28% of our
vocabulary, of which 22.2% is accounted for by Anglo-Saxon. The
remaining 4.08% breaks down as follows: Scandinavian 2.16%; Low
German (including Dutch and Frisian) 1.42%; High German, as we
have seen, 0.5%. (I shall return to the question of Low German
later.) A small, but not insignificant contribution, then, and
one that has been particularly important for certain areas of
the English vocabulary.

In preparing my survey in 1969 I found that the field had not been intensively researched. The standard histories of English made reference to German influence, but were unable to deal with the subject in any depth. (Since then, Barbara Strang's *History of English* (1970) has appeared, and that work accords our topic more than usually generous treatment, though given the nature of her book - it is a chronological account, notorious in that it works from the present-day backwards - the inquirer has to hunt the passages out.) On the other hand, the two works which do devote themselves exclusively to the subject of borrowing into English, M.S. Sergeantson's *History of Foreign Words in English* (1935) and A.J. Bliss's *Dictionary of Foreign Words and Phrases* (1966) rule out more than superficial treatment by virtue of encompassing the whole gamut of borrowing. In fact there was, and still is, only one published monograph on the subject. This is by the late C.T. Carr, and it appeared as Tract 42 of the 'Society for Pure English' in 1934. Despite its name, the Society is not a British equivalent of the 'Allgemeiner deutscher Sprach-verein', and was responsible for publishing a number of monographs on the foreign elements of our vocabulary of a scholarly and thoroughly reputable nature. Carr's monograph is not long; in 60 pages he lists 820 German loan-words and loan-translations taken largely from the *OED*, which work had been completed the previous year. The material is listed chronologically by period, and within each period by topic. There is a very short introduction alerting the reader to differences between *aliens* and *denizens*, and between loan-words and loan-translations. Otherwise any text is confined to introducing each period and pointing up the cultural influences giving rise to the borrowings. The words are then listed alphabetically, with date of first appearance and brief notes on the original German term, the route taken into the language etc. Carr supplemented his list in 1940 in an article in *MLR*; here he added 20 further items to his collection and corrected several datings.

From this description it will have become clear that Carr's work, while valuable in excerpting the material from the *OED*, is

exclusively concerned with historical matters. He is interested
in earliest datings, and he is interested in the historical and
cultural influences leading to the borrowings. And there the
matter rested, apart from a few articles which offered nothing
new, until 1961, when Klaus Schäfer wrote an *Examensarbeit* (unpublished) for Heidelberg University. While Schäfer's work relies
heavily on Carr, and thus on the *OED*, it does include sections on
the phonetic and graphemic adaptation and assimilation of the
German material.

Such was the *Stand der Forschung* in 1968. I was able then,
in the time and space available to me, to knot together the two
themes, the full tide of Anglicisms flowing into German and the
far weaker countercurrent from German into English. But I was
aware that, as far as this latter aspect was concerned, two main
Forschungslücken remained. First, I had only been able to
indicate that borrowing from German had been continuing after
1933, the year the *OED* was published: there was much lexicological spade-work to be done for the war years and beyond. Second,
the emphasis hitherto had been on the diachronic and topical
approach: synchrony had been almost entirely neglected.

Spending the academic year 1970/71 teaching at the University
of Wisconsin at Madison I worked alongside a former *Sprachatlas*
colleague, Jürgen Eichhoff, who was researching the related, though
more complex, question of the German influence on AE. We decided
to pool our resources and are now preparing a full-scale study
for the Erich Schmidt Verlag. Although on my side work has been
delayed by the day-to-day exigencies familiar to British university
teachers, the welcome prospect of sabbatical leave leads me to
hope that the study will be completed early in 1984. With the
possibility of taking up intensive work on the project again after
a period during which it has necessarily lain dormant, I am
especially grateful for this chance to dust off my scribblings
and to benefit not only from thinking the topic through again,
but also from subjecting my ideas to your scrutiny and criticism.

In order that this paper may be informative for all concerned, that is for both listeners and speaker, I propose firstly to outline the main periods and topics of borrowing up to the present: this will form the largest part of the paper. Secondly I shall relate this historical, topical account to the overall structure of the project; and thirdly I shall point to some theoretical and methodological problems where discussion might profitably begin.

German influence on the English vocabulary started around 1520 as a direct result of the Reformation, and it has continued up to the present time. Before the Reformation, it is true, linguistic contacts may be identified, but these were of a different order.

Firstly, was there any influence from OHG on OE, given that the traffic was so heavy in the opposite direction as a result of the Anglo-Saxon mission? Werner Betz (1949 : 99 and 208) thought that there was: he established one loan-word proper (OE *cugle* < OHG *cucala* < Lat. *cuculla* 'monk's cowl'); further, ten religious and two secular loan-renderings. Betz attributed these borrowings to the Benedictine reforms of Dunstan and Aethelwold in the tenth century, with the monastery of Fleury playing a mediating rôle. However, subsequently Helmut Gneuss (1955 : 93) has shown that OHG origin is not possible in the case of four of these, and that the remaining nine might just as well be independent coinings in OE. Equally unclear is the way in which four Greek religious terms - *dēofol, enġel, ċiriċe* 'church' and *prēost* - and one Latin term, *hæðen* 'heathen' - came into English. The Gothic mission in Germany has been proposed, but proof is elusive.

We do know, however, that OHG had an *indirect* influence on OE as a result of the Norman conquest. In particular, terms relating to warfare, hunting, heraldry and law had been adopted by Old French, and these were then brought to the British Isles: e.g. NE *garb* < OHG *garawi* 'armour'; NE *robe* < OHG *roub* 'spolia' - the armour forfeited by the vanquished opponent. Indeed, some of these terms displaced established native etymological equi-

valents.   Thus NE *blue* < OFr. *bleu* < OHG *blāo*, with OE *blā* dying
out; *robe* we have just seen to derive ultimately from OHG *roub*,
but OE had the cognate *rēaf*, and the verb *rēafian* 'to steal'.
This word type now only lives on in the term *to bereave*.

Leaving the earliest attested periods of contact we must consider the question of contacts which took place before the starting
point I mentioned earlier, namely the Reformation.   The significant fact here is that the bulk of the borrowings came from Low
German (LG) and Dutch.   The cultural and mercantile traffic was
predominantly with the Netherlands and the Hansa, and much borrowing resulted.   That is why the proportion of Dutch and LG borrowings is so much higher in the figures I quoted above (1.42% as
against 0.5%).   There is just one word that we can point to with
any certainty as being from HG before 1500, and that is the mining
term *glance* in the compound *glance-ore*, which English borrowed in
1458 from Dutch *glans*, and which Dutch had taken from HG *glanz*.
It is of significance that this, the first known HG word in
English came from an area of technology that was later to provide
a very large number of terms.

With the Reformation we have the first wave of unambiguously
HG borrowings - the historical impulse is known, the channels of
transmission identifiable.   And yet - the Reformation provides
us with a good example of the fact that although borrowing is the
result of cultural influence, it is not true to say that the
amount of borrowing is dependent on the degree of influence exerted.
In comparison with the significance that the Reformation had for
the British Isles, the number of borrowings it occasioned is very
small indeed.   Carr (1934 : 40) found a mere ten in the *OED:*
papist, Romanist, silverling, weakling, mercy seat, shewbread,
Anabaptist, Protestant and *sinflood.*   Only *weakling, Anabaptist,*
Protestant and *papist* have survived.   *Romanist* nowadays means
'scholar of the Romance languages and literatures' and was coined
(or revived) in the 19th century by analogy to *Anglist* and
Germanist.

More numerous than the words entering NE as a result of the
Reformation and the activities of the Bible translators are a
series of botanical items. These were introduced by William
Turner (*Names of Herbes*, 1578; *A New Herball*, 1551) and Henry
Lyte (*Nieuwe Herball*, 1548). Here again, however, the difficulty
of separating HG from Dutch influence presents itself, since we
know that Turner travelled extensively in the Low Countries as
well as in Germany, and Lyte's book is a re-working of the
Cruydeboek by the Flemish botanist Rembert Dodoens von Mechlin.
We can be sure of some terms, however, such as *larch* (< *Lärche*
and *digitalis*, a Latinisation by the German botanist Fuchs of NHG
Fingerhut.

A handful of other words came into English during the sixteenth century, but indirectly, through intermediary languages,
and thus have suffered some distortion: e.g. before the loan
translation *lance-knight* was replaced by the loan-word *landsknecht*,
it was partnered by a French form *lansquenet*; the verb *to carouse*
reached us via French, too: its ultimate form was *gar aus trinken*;
fife is a French form of NHG *Pfeife*; *halt* (1591) came to us from
German via Spanish *alto*.

Despite the immense significance, then, of the Reformation,
intercourse between Germany and Britain was not sufficiently
intensive to produce a flow of borrowings comparable to those
arriving in Britain from the Low Countries, and the majority of
loans that did come here travelled 'on the backs' of other languages.

With the seventeenth century the importance of German scientific and technical terms for the English vocabulary becomes evident,
whereby we must remember that some of the borrowings are not themselves German but Neo-Latin. Paracelsus' terms *laudanum*,
salamander, *sylph* and *undine* entered English at this time, as did
Kepler's coinings *dioptrical*, *focus*, *inertia* and *satellite*. One
might argue that this is less a case of German influence on
English, but rather of the German contribution to the international language of science.

With the other main area of technical influence, mining,
the situation is quite different: here German influence is
direct and in many cases oral. German miners had first been
brought to these shores in the 13th century to work the Cornish
tin mines. In the 16th century the British government negotiated
with German mining companies with a view to getting superior
German expertise to exploit British iron deposits. I quote
details from Schäfer (1961 : 30):

> 'Die Erschließung der Kupfererze des Lake District und
> der Erze von Northumberland wurde in Angriff genommen,
> zum Teil unter Beteiligung deutschen Kapitals. 1563
> wurde in Keswick eine deutsche Bergwerksgesellschaft
> gegründet und kamen 300-400 deutsche Bergarbeiter nach
> Cumberland. Nachdem die Cumberlandminen 1579 von den
> Engländern übernommen wurden, wurden deutsche Berg-
> arbeiter auch zur Erschließung von Blei-, Kupfer- und
> Silbergruben in Cornwall eingesetzt ... Die Hebung
> des englischen Bergbaus mit deutscher Hilfe setzte
> sich auch ins 17. Jahrhundert hinein fort. Jakob I.
> ließ deutsche Bergleute zum Abbau der Bleierze York-
> shires und der Silbererze Durhams anwerben, und Prinz
> Rupert soll deutsche Fachleute nach Ecton/Staffordshire
> geholt haben, um die Verwendung von Schießpulver im
> Bergbau vorzuführen.'

The first written evidence of borrowings in the area of mining
dates from the 17th century, even though we may assume that oral
borrowing had taken place in the previous century. *Cobalt* and
zinc are examples that have remained current. We shall see
that the German mineralogical and geological terms will enter the
language in increased numbers during the two succeeding centuries.
The importance of German in this field may be seen in the fact
that, at least until recently, many British university students
of geology, mineralogy and metallurgy had to pass examinations in
German. Indeed, C.T. Carr (1934 : 89) saw this interest in
German mineralogy as being instrumental in paving the way for a
more general interest in things German in the 19th century:

> 'In the sciences the influence of the German nomenclature
> of mineralogy and geology is the oldest, and has remained
> the most constant. The importance of this influence on
> the general cultural relations between Germany and England
> cannot be estimated too highly. A knowledge of German
> was indispensable to English mineralogists about 1800,

and they were the forerunners and pioneers of that
awakening of interest in the German language and
German thought which came about the time of Scott,
Coleridge and Carlyle'.

Before moving on to the 18th century I must mention that a
few military terms entered English from German as a result of wars,
notably the Thirty Years War, if only because among them is a
Czech borrowing for Dr. Martin's collection.   This is *Haubitz*,
English *howitzer*.   To the same period belong *fieldmarshall*,
plunder and the semantic loan *staff*.   Also of interest is the
term *spanner*, which was borrowed in 1639 in the sense 'Federspanner
bei Schußwaffen' but subsequently widened to its modern sense
'Schraubenschlüssel'.

Finally, the entry of the first two culinary terms from
German must be noted.   *Hock* is of interest as a clipping (from
Hochheimer) and also as an example of phonemic substitution
($[x] > [k]$), while *sauerkraut* provided Americans with a term of
abuse for the whole nation (*Kraut*).

It is perhaps surprising that, although the number of
Germanisms entering English increased in the 18th century, this
did not happen until the second half of that century - surprising
since in 1714 George the First ascended the throne, which remained
in Hanoverian possession until the death of William IV in 1837.
In 1714, then, the English entered, to quote R.J. White (1967 :
194), 'the long flat plain of the Hanoverian Age, the happiest
if not the noblest era of its modern history'.   But George I
couldn't speak English, and even his son George II (1727-60) is
said to have had a thick German accent.   We can get a picture
of the Babel that must have been prevalent at court as a result
of the international marriage market from a comment - admittedly
dating from the 19th century - attributed to Princess Charlotte,
the daughter of the Duke of Brunswick and daughter-in-law of
George III: 'And when I did look round at them I said to myself,
"A quoi bon this dull assemblage of tiresome persons ... *Mein Gott!*
Dat is de dullest person Gott Almighty ever did born"' (Bryant,
1954 : 105).   The fact that the monarch couldn't speak his

subjects' language did not seem to cause difficulty. After all, he could speak French at court, and indeed, as Carr (1934 : 50) points out, the preeminence of French in the 18th century in both Germany and England probably accounts for the relatively limited flow of borrowings until the second half of the century, when the number of mineralogical and geological terms increased drama- tically. Most of these are still in use, but in technical registers; more widely known are *graphite, nickel* (via Swedish), *quartz,* this last item having recently become a household word as a result of the application of quartz to timepiece technology. From this period stem the miscellaneous terms *homesickness,* a trans- lation of the Swiss-German term *Heimweh, pumpernickel, waltz, statistics* and *swindler*.

With the 19th century we come to the high water mark of German borrowing into English. If we take both of Carr's col- lections together we obtain a total of 840 Germanisms entering English between 1458 and 1935. 474 - over half - of these entered during the 19th century, and most of them during two short periods: between 1830 and 1850 under Carlyle's influence, and between 1870 and 1890, when the majority of borrowings were scientific and technical.

The scientific vocabulary - much of it in Greek and Latin disguise - may be divided into the following categories:

1. the traditional area of geology and mineralogy,
   e.g. *watershed, triassic*;

2. chemistry, e.g. *morphine, biochemical, saccharine, aspirin*;

3. physics, e.g. *spectrometer, dynamo, x-rays*;

4. medicine, e.g. *bacterium, streptococcus, tuberculin*;

5. biology, e.g. the word *biology* itself, *edelweiss, plankton*;

6. psychology, e.g. *suppression,* a translation of Wundt's term *Verdrängung*.

In the arts and humanities we see the borrowed material
clustering under the heads of literature, philosophy, philology
and pedagogy. In these areas the number of words made up of
German elements is greater. Literary influence in the 19th
century is associated first with the mediation of Henry Mackenzie
and Walter Scott; secondly with the reception of Mme. de Staël's
book on Germany and with Thomas Carlyle; thirdly with Matthew
Arnold. Among the terms borrowed are *dramaturgy, mastersinger,
philistine, storm and stress* and *time-spirit*, these latter two
nowadays more frequently occurring in their untranslated form.

Most of the philosophical vocabulary from German takes the
form of semantic loans - thus Kant's terms: *form, idea, intuition,
reason, understanding*. An appropriate example to illustrate
philological influence is the loan-translation *loan-word*, which
dates from 1874, while education may be represented by the terms
kindergarten, seminar and *semester*, this last especially in AE.

It is surprising that the strong influence of German music
has not led to more terms being borrowed. Those that have come
- e.g. *kapellmeister, concert-master, chorale, schottische* (pro-
nounced as if French), *alpenhorn, glockenspiel, leitmotiv* (also
-if, reflecting French mediation) - occur with great frequency.
It would seem that English music terminology had already been
largely formed under Italian influence. We must remember that
when Georg Friedrich Händel came to England in the 18th century
he immediately lost his *umlaut* (a philological loan-word from
1860!) and was thereupon considered by the English to be their
greatest national composer. But Handel, as I must now call him,
espoused the Italian musical tradition.

The twentieth century falls, as far as this present survey
is concerned, into two parts - the period up to 1933, when the
OED and its *Supplement* appeared, providing Carr, Schäfer and
others with the collected material for their studies, and the
period from 1933 to the present time. For this period we are
obliged to seek our material elsewhere; the new *OED Supplement*
is a help, but is still uncompleted.

In the period up to the First World War the nature and scale of the borrowing was similar to that of the previous few decades. The First World War itself appears to have produced more new German terms into English than the Second did. Although the following words are mostly used in connection with the Second World War they were all borrowed during the First: *ersatz*, *flame-thrower*, *mine-thrower*, *shock-troops*, *to strafe*, *U-boat*. (The verb *to strafe* has, in British English, preserved the German vowel pronunciation [ɑ:], while in American English the pronunciate accords with 'normal' rules as [ei].) Although the number of Germanisms entering British English has never been sufficient to provoke puristic chauvinism, an early citation of the loan-word *schadenfreude* quoted by the *OED Supplement* (1933) from the *Spectator* (24th July 1926) reveals a certain insular priggishness: 'There is no English word for *Schadenfreude*, because there is no such feeling here.'

In an attempt to measure the extent of borrowing after 1933, as well as the frequency of the borrowed items, I excerpted the British press over a longer period unsystematically, and for a short period systematically. The results of these searches have appeared elsewhere (Stanforth, 1974). Suffice it to say here that I found 114 German loan-words and loan-translations not recorded in the *OED*. This material includes journalistic nonce-words unlikely to be repeated; for example: *schräge Musik* in the following:

> 'but as a good German he cannot resist his moments of
> *schadenfreude* when an enemy aircraft is in the gun-
> sights, or when the *schräge Musik* from a night-fighter's
> obliquely mounted guns is ripping into the vulnerable
> under-belly of a Lancaster bomber'
> (*The Times*, Nov. 4th, 1967).

Nevertheless, one has to be careful about deciding too quickly what will stay and what will disappear, indeed, about making any kind of predictions. C.T. Carr (1940 : 71), for instance, registered *putsch* in 1940, glossing it as 'coup d'état' but commenting:

'It appears to be spreading to English slang in the non-
political significance of a "push forward". See
Alice Campbell, *Flying Blind* (1938), p.89: "He
grasped it firmly and flexing his muscles prepared a
putsch."'

The 114 items can be allotted to the following categories:

1. Politics (32), e.g. *Bundestag, diktat, lebensraum*;

2. Food (13), e.g. *bratwurst, eisbein, nusstorte*;

3. Warfare (10), e.g. *abwehr, blitzkrieg, sitzkrieg*;

4. The Arts, excluding music (9), e.g. *bildungsroman,
    kitsch, stegreifkomödie*;

5. Music (6), e.g. *flugelhorn, lieder, gebrauchsmusik*;

6. Economics (4), e.g. *Deutschmarks, gastarbeiter*;

7. Miscellaneous (40), e.g. *abseiling, federbett, wunderkind*.

Not all the items collected are modern. *Bildungsroman* and *lieder*,
for instance, will have been borrowed well before the *OED* was
compiled but were simply missed.   The large number of political
words reflects the nature of my source - the press.   But nevertheless both Carr (1934 : 86) and Schäfer (1961) pointed to a
growing number of political terms entering English from German.

Writing the conclusion of his survey Carr (1934 : 89)
explained the relative paucity of German loans in English with
the words: ' ... there has been no great event in German history
which has appealed to the imagination of the English as the French
Revolution did.' While he was writing those words the events
were developing which were to influence the British view of Germany
and things German in a more far-reaching way than any previous
event, not excluding the First World War.   Of the 32 political
words referred to, nine are unequivocally Nazi terms.   Indeed,
the word *Nazi* itself is one of the most frequent of all Germanisms
in English.   Moreover, most of the military terms derive from
the trauma of the Thirties and Forties.   Only *Bundestag* post-
dates the war.   I have already indicated that the number of
military words entering English during the First World War (or
as a result of it) seems higher.   But for British ears words
such as *panzer, total war* and *blitzkrieg* exert an awful potency,

a potency which goes some way towards explaining why the clipping *blitz* has become one of the most productive new words in the English language.

On the other hand, the number of technical terms is not large. In fact, the material comprises only one - *angst*. This term has by now freed itself from the technical language of psychology and is widely used by laymen, especially in compounds such as *angst-ridden*. The dearth of new scientific borrowings may be a reflection of the growing importance of English as an international scientific language in the twentieth century. On the other hand it is worth noting that I have been able to set up a category not needed by Carr: that is the category 'Economics'. Constantly the British reader is reminded in his newspaper of the strength of the *D—Mark*, the *Deutschmark*, the *deutsche-Mark*, the *German mark* ... And he dreams of a British *wirtschaftswunder*.

What you have heard up to this point represents a traditional, historical account of periods of influence and the resultant borrowings. When assessing the influence of a language such as German on a language such as English the primary interest must surely be: which words have entered the language, and what were the cultural factors that led to the borrowing? As Sapir (1921 : 192) put it: 'Languages, like cultures, are rarely sufficient unto themselves ... The careful study of ... loan-words constitutes an interesting commentary on the history of culture.' Nevertheless, while older works generally stopped at that point, much remains to be said about such matters as 1) the linguistic classification of the loan-material; 2) the assimilation of the borrowed vocabulary; 3) purism; 4) frequency of use; 5) rate of loss. At this stage, i.e. of my work on the project and of the time left to me today, I can do little more than place the historical account just outlined in the context of the work as a whole.

The book is to be divided into two main sections, of which the first, consisting of two chapters, is introductory. Chapter 1 describes the subject to be treated, chapter 2 the theoretical

background. The second section commences with the historical
account (chap. 3), and this is followed by seven further chapters
dealing with (4) specific problems relating to the influence of
German on American English, e.g. the question of intimate borrowing
from German as an immigrant language; (5) the question of Yiddish,
especially in the United States; one recalls Leo Rosten's comment:
'It is a remarkable fact that never in its history has Yiddish
been so influential - among Gentiles' (1970 : xi).   Chapters 5,
6 and 7 treat aspects of the linguistic assimilation of the
Germanisms (pronunciation, orthography, Syntax and morphology,
semantic development); chapter 9 is concerned with functional
and stylistic aspects of the use of Germanisms, and the final
chapter attempts an evaluation of the influence in terms of relative proportion of the overall lexicon, number of items in everyday use, frequency of use; it will also examine what evidence
there may be for influences that are not reflected in the vocabulary.

Each of these areas could provide material enough for a
separate paper and throw up many questions suitable for discussion
at a conference such as the present one.   I should like to conclude at this point by picking out several problem areas on which
I should especially welcome discussion:

1. the lack of a fully satisfactory theory of borrowing.
    Traditional, much criticised terminologies such as
    Werner Betz' scheme *versus*, e.g. the linguistically
    more rigorous but tiresomely opaque terminology of
    Lüllwitz;

2. the *mechanisms* of borrowing; identifying the point
    when individual usage is accepted as part of *langue*;

3. is total synchrony possible?   Is a word-field approach
    possible?

References

Auburger, L. & Kloss, H. (eds.) (1977) *Deutsch als Muttersprache
    in Kanada.* Wiesbaden, Steiner.

Auburger, L. & Kloss, H. (eds.) (1979) *Deutsche Sprachkontakte
    in Übersee.* Tübingen, Narr.

Betz, W. (1949) *Deutsch und Lateinisch. Die Lehnbildungen der
    althochdeutschen Benediktiner Regel.* Bonn.

Betz, W. (1944) 'Die Lehnbildungen und der abendländische Sprach-
enausgleich' *Beiträge zur Geschichte der deutschen Sprache
und Literatur* 67: 275-302.

Bliss, A.J. (1966) *Dictionary of Foreign Words and Phrases*.
London.

Bryant, A. (1954) *The Age of Elegance*. London, Reprint Society.

Burchfield, R.W. (1972) *The Oxford English Dictionary. Supplement I, A-G*. Oxford, OUP.

Carr, C.T. (1934) *The German Influence on the English Vocabulary*
(S.P.E. Tract, 42). Oxford.

Carr, C.T. (1940) 'Some Notes on German Loan Words in English'
Modern Language Review 35: 69-71.

Finkenstaedt, Th. & Wolff, D. (1973) *Ordered Profusion - Studies
in Dictionaries and the English Lexicon*. Heidelberg.

Gneuss, H. (1955) *Lehnbildungen und Lehnbedeutungen im Alten-
glischen*. Berlin.

Kloss, H. (1978) *Die Entwicklung neuer germanischer Kultursprachen seit 1800*. Düsseldorf, Schwann.

Lüllwitz, B. (1972) 'Interferenz und Transferenz' *Germanistische
Linguistik* 2/72: 159-291.

Mitzka, W. (ed.) (1968) *Wortgeographie und Gesellschaft*. Berlin,
de Gruyter.

Molony, C. *et al.* (1977) *German in Contact with Other Languages*.
Kronberg, Scriptor.

Murray, J.A.H. *et al.* (1933) *The Oxford English Dictionary*.
Oxford, OUP.

Nelde, P.H. (ed.) (1980) *Sprachkontakt und Sprachkonflikt* (ZDL
Beihefte, 32). Wiesbaden, Steiner.

Onions, C.T. *et al.* (1964) *The Shorter Oxford English Dictionary*.
Oxford, OUP.

Rosten, L. (1970) *The Joys of Yiddish*. New York, Pocket Book.

Sampson, A. (1968) *The New Europeans*. London.

Sapir, E. (1921) *Language*. New York, Harcourt, Brace and World.

Schäfer, K. (1961) *Das deutsche Wortgut im Neuenglischen*
(unpublished dissertation). Heidelberg.

Scheler, M. (1977) *Der englische Wortschatz*. Berlin, Schmidt.

Sergeantson, M.S. (1935) *A History of Foreign Words in English*.
London.

Stanforth, A.W. (1974) 'Lexical Borrowing from German since 1933
as Reflected in the British Press' *The Modern Language
Review* 69: 325-36.

Strang, B.M.H. (1970) *A History of English*. London, Methuen.

White, R.J. (1967) *A Short History of England*. Cambridge, CUP.